WHAT'S WRONG

WHAT'S WRONG

Understanding sin today

MIKE STARKEY

Text copyright © Mike Starkey 2001
The author asserts the moral right
to be identified as the author of this work

Published by
The Bible Reading Fellowship
First Floor, Elsfield Hall
15–17 Elsfield Way, Oxford OX2 8FG
ISBN 1 84101 152 5

First published 2001
10 9 8 7 6 5 4 3 2 1 0
All rights reserved

A catalogue record for this book is available from the British Library

Printed and bound in Great Britain by
Omnia Books Limited, Glasgow

Contents

Introduction   6

1 Exit Sin   10

2 Sceptical about the Secular Sceptics   30

3 Critical of the Christian Critics   55

4 Adam, Eve and Origins   79

5 Passing It On   108

6 The Rescue Operation   128

Introduction

Why bother writing a book on something as unpopular, and apparently outdated, as the Christian doctrine of sin? The origins of this book lie mainly in a series of conversations I have had over recent years.

Having written earlier books on fashion and identity (*Fashion and Style*, Monarch, 1995) and rediscovering the wonder of life (*God, Sex & Generation X* and *Restoring the Wonder*, Triangle, 1997 and 1999), I found myself being invited to speak on these subjects, particularly to groups of students and other young adults. Inevitably, conversations turn to wider issues than image and wonder. Sooner or later, we get on to the really big questions: questions of who God is, and what Christians believe (theology), and questions of how we make decisions affecting our behaviour and lifestyle (ethics). Time after time, it becomes clear that the people with whom I am chatting have quite clearly formed opinions on both topics, even those who claim no religious commitment. And these opinions generally go something like this...

In terms of faith, these young adults almost always draw a sharp line between religion—or the institutional Church—and spirituality. Spirituality is seen as private, individual, creative and liberating. The Church, on the other hand, is seen as external, corporate, stifling creativity, and oppressive or coercive. Spirituality is something personally felt and experienced at the level of heart and senses, while the Church is seen as dealing in impersonal doctrines. Spirituality is for real people, theology for socially maladjusted boffins. Spirituality makes you interesting, theology makes you boring.

Similar distinctions are made in the area of ethics. An open, laid-back attitude is pitted against a rigid, authoritarian ethic of rule-keeping. Contemporary culture is associated with tolerance, while the institutional Church is associated with legalism. Contemporary culture is seen as open and accepting of diversity, while the Church is seen as closed and judgmental. Attitudes like these are simply accepted as the new common sense, even by young people raised to attend church, and many who are happy to describe themselves as Christians.

There is one big idea, close to the heart of historic Christian belief, which touches on both these areas, theology and ethics. It is the doctrine of sin. But mention the word 'sin' to these young adults, and it is clear where they will locate it on their mental maps. In the battle between religion and spirituality, it is firmly on the side of religion. And in the battle between tolerance and judgmentalism, it falls equally firmly on the side of judgmentalism. Little surprise, then, that the doctrine of sin has been all but dropped from the vocabulary of many churches, and appears only rarely in general conversation (usually in connection with cream cakes or kinky sex, and spoken with a twinkle in the eye). The whole idea feels archaic, intolerant and morbid. For most young adults today, the only real 'sin' is being intolerant of others' lifestyle choices.

The technical term for doing theology within the community of faith, showing how the different bits fit together and how each fits in with scripture, is *dogmatics*. And the term for explaining and defending the faith to unbelievers and sceptics is *apologetics*. This is not really a book of dogmatics, although I do try to unpack some of the big issues surrounding the theology of sin. It is more a book of apologetics—an attempt to defend the biblical idea of sin, and explain why historic Christianity has always found in it a profound truth and value unobtainable elsewhere. And it is a book that tries to point out where the popular mindset of the day (as expressed by those students and young adults with whom I've been having chats) is flawed and inadequate.

Here is what I believe: that theology is simply spirituality with the brain engaged; that believing in sin is something positive and life-affirming, that makes for saner people and happier societies; and that the Church, for all its problems, remains something fascinating and wonderful. I make no apologies that these beliefs contradict almost everything my contemporaries assume to be true, and most of the opinions they will have encountered in college, media and home.

Here is something else I believe: that it is an exhilarating time to be a defender of orthodox Christianity. Western culture has largely come through its post-Christian phase, and is now out on the other side. Today, we are closer to the situation of the early Church—addressing a pre-Christian culture with a strange, new message. Like the Church of the first century, we are again faced with a culture which is sophisticated, urban and decadent, whose main belief-system is a laid-back and tolerant pluralism. We are confronting such a culture with a gospel that is new, startling, and offensively exclusive in its claims. To most people, such a gospel will seem threatening and subversive—which, of course, it is.

This book is an attempt to restate the biblical doctrine of sin in a way that connects with a contemporary mindset. My aim has been, on the one hand, to be faithful to the biblical evidence and the witness of the Christian tradition and, on the other, open to the new questions and fresh challenges of our day. I have been motivated by reverence for the Bible as divine revelation, but have felt freer to question the Church's own interpretations of that revelation, and its practice down the centuries.

In writing this book, I have obviously had to dialogue with great Christian thinkers of the past, particularly the apostle Paul and Augustine, Bishop of Hippo in North Africa in the late 4th and early 5th centuries. I am (as always) indebted to those giants of 20th-century popular Christian writing, G.K. Chesterton and C.S. Lewis. The contemporary thinkers whose work I found consistently helpful as I thought through the issues addressed in the book included Donald Bloesch, Stanley Grenz, Mary Midgley, Clark Pinnock, R.J. Berry, Henri Blocher, Michael Lloyd, John Drane and Tom Smail. Thanks to Tom Smail, Anne Holmes and John Davis for reading an early version of the manuscript and offering helpful comments. Needless to say, any shortcomings are my own responsibility, and can't be blamed (in true 'Adamic' style) on anybody else.

Inevitably, some readers will feel that key thinkers and ideas are touched on all too briefly here. They will be frustrated that some great theologians are dismissed, or given a thumbs-up, on the basis of a single statement. They will feel short-changed because I don't say enough about the details of ethical decision-making, or go into enough detail on what the 'sanctified' Christian life might look like. To all this I plead guilty as charged. In defence, I can only say that these are issues for another day. This book is designed as an introduction. It is intended not as a comprehensive or final word, but as a stimulus to further thought and discussion.

One friend recently commented that he thought I was the ideal person to write a book on sin. I'm still not sure whether or not that was a compliment.

CHAPTER 1

Exit sin

> 'That seems to me so evil that it's beyond my understanding.
> Alice, what you did was a dreadful sin.'
> Alice laughed... 'Meg, you continue to astonish me. You use
> words which are no longer in the general vocabulary, not even in
> the Church's, so I'm told. The implications of that simple little
> word are beyond my comprehension.'
>
> P.D. JAMES, *DEVICES AND DESIRES*

> There is one thing a professor can be absolutely certain of; almost
> every student entering the university believes, or says he believes,
> that truth is relative... That anyone should regard the proposition
> as not self-evident astonishes them.
>
> ALLAN BLOOM, *THE CLOSING OF THE AMERICAN MIND*

> No two people see events the same way. Everybody's truth
> is different.
>
> GERI HALLIWELL, *IF ONLY*

Fire and brimstone in New England

The scene: a small church in the town of Enfield, Connecticut. The date: 8 July, 1741. The preacher: Jonathan Edwards, the 38-year-old Congregational minister from the nearby town of Northampton. Edwards had not originally been due to preach in Enfield that Sunday evening, but agreed to stand in for another man. The congregation sits with no great sense of expectation, listless, complacent.

The visiting preacher has decided to reuse a sermon he had preached in his own church a few weeks earlier. The sermon and its delivery style are both uncharacteristic for the academic Edwards, who is more used to extolling the beauties of Christ or writing philosophical essays. Today he delivers a blistering account of the sinfulness of humanity and the divine wrath. His title is 'Sinners in the Hands of an Angry God', his text Deuteronomy 32:35: 'It is mine to avenge; I will repay. In due time their foot will slip; their day of disaster is near and their doom rushes upon them.'

Ignoring the congregation's apathetic yawns, Edwards shifts into overdrive:

The God that holds you over the pit of hell, much as one holds a spider or some loathsome insect over the fire, abhors you and is dreadfully provoked. His wrath towards you burns like fire... You have offended him infinitely more than ever a stubborn rebel did his prince—and yet it is nothing but his hand that holds you from falling into the fire every moment.

According to contemporary eye-witnesses, the effect of Jonathan Edwards' sermon is electrifying. One writes how the congregation, before the sermon is ended, are 'bowed down with an awful conviction of their sin and danger'. Another writes in his diary for that Sunday that Edwards' sermon is constantly interrupted by members of the congregation, screaming and crying out to God in repentance.

By the end of the evening, an extraordinary sense of peace and joy has descended on the members of that Enfield church. This time, however, it is not the quiet indifference that characterized the early evening. It is the exhausted, cathartic joy of people who have stared destruction in the teeth and escaped with their lives, breathless and relieved.

Jonathan Edwards' sermon would become one of the most famous ever preached. It was a crucial catalyst for the massive Christian revival which spread across 18th-century New England, known as the Great Awakening. Edwards, a convinced Calvinist, was a man deeply conscious of the grandeur and holiness of God, and of humanity's sinfulness and hopelessness without divine grace. This became a major focus of the Awakening: an almost physical sensation of being weighed down by a burden of sin; a very real terror of eternal perdition, since our sin cuts us off from a holy Creator; then an extraordinary sense of release on grasping for the first time the good news that Jesus Christ died for our sins, an unspeakable joy at restored fellowship with God.

In Puritan New England, sin is no armchair theological debate. Sin and its remedy are as real as the bread on the table and the rooster in the barnyard. They are the stuff of screams, tears and ecstasy—eternally significant, passionately real.

Sex and cream cakes

Poor Jonathan Edwards. I sometimes imagine him returning to present-day Enfield, Connecticut, or maybe Enfield, north London. Or Stock-holm, Sydney or Cape Town. I picture him entering one of our churches, or perhaps the seating area of a shopping mall, and launching into a stirring rerun of 'Sinners in the Hands of an Angry God'. And I picture the looks on people's faces: the wry grins, the condescending looks, the sniggers and exchanged glances.

Today we are wiser, more urbane and more cosmopolitan than the townsfolk of 18th-century New England. We know what's what. And sin is no longer a part of our vocabulary, at least, not a part of our regular vocabulary. We have limited the idea of sin to three rather narrow areas.

The first of these is sexuality, particularly sex in the seaside-postcard, nudge-nudge-wink-wink, hanky-panky zone. The tabloid press still reserves the word 'sin' for its frequent exposés of celebrities' sexual peccadilloes. The word carries a sense of shock and censure, but in a way which smiles indulgently at the same time. When we use the word 'sin' we are affecting moral disapproval, but in a way which rather enjoys contemplating the sin in question. One of the few English phrases to retain the word sin is 'living in sin', a euphemism for extra-marital cohabitation. But even that usage is going out of use as cohabitation is seen increasingly as the norm for young couples. As the *frisson* of transgression is fading, so too is our need to use the term 'sin'.

A second use of the word 'sin' is to define areas of life where we know we ought to have more self-control, but constantly find ourselves slipping into temptation. But here, too, the use of the term 'sin' implies an indulgent, good-humoured censure, such as our response to the temptation offered by cream cakes. We know we shouldn't, but it does look *so* delicious. And just think of all those calories. Oh go on, just this once. I *do* feel naughty! The vocabulary of sin regularly finds its way into the marketing of high-calorie, self-indulgent foods.

Our third use of 'sin' parodies archaic religious attitudes. The Pet Shop Boys' song 'It's a Sin' looks back on a repressive religious up-bringing with regret. Every time a different memory of childhood initiative or pleasure surfaces, so does a stern parental and ecclesiastical response: 'It's a sin!' This attempt to caricature the religiosity of an earlier era explains the frequent use of the word in the lyrics of heavy metal music. Sin-laden lyrics evoke a gothic mood and sense of trans-gression, with a slight hint at sexuality.

A common idiom in contemporary English uses the language of sin in a humorous and self-deprecating way: 'Is it true you've been elected president of the organization?' 'Yes, for my sins!' This type of response bears closer scrutiny. It too evokes an earlier era of stern, finger-wagging moralists. But it does so with irony and a twinkle in the eye. We joke that our present fortune is in fact a punishment for some past misdeeds. It is a witticism that only works because we and our hearer know full well that neither part of the equation is true: our current status is actually a welcome one and, in any case, there is no cosmic law of retribution for our wrongdoings. We can play with the sin language of a bygone era, confident in the knowledge that it will not turn around and bite us: it has no teeth.

At the time of writing, a magazine advertisement for Saab cars bears the title 'Saab vs the Puritans'. It lampoons a common stereotype of the puritanical attitude to pleasure: 'It is sinful to seek any form of pleasure. Overt joy is to be avoided. Do not drive a Saab 9-3 Convertible… just looking at the car's sleek shape could be considered lustful. Be careful, modern-day Puritans. Who knows what this car could lead to?'

Again note the wry, ironic tone. The same message is reinforced: sin, like a sepia-toned photo of the comic actor Buster Keaton, is old-fashioned and humorous. Sin, like kinky sex and cream cakes, is harmless self-indulgence. And with the widespread lifting of the taboo against cohabitation, even the phrase 'living in sin' is only used by most people in an ironic, playful way that satirizes the moralizing of an earlier era: 'Ooh, so you two are living in sin! Ha ha!'

In particular, Puritanism and traditional Catholicism are held up as the ultimate in quaint, outdated belief-systems, due to their prioritizing of sin. So negative! So repressive! But now we have broken away from their rusty old shackles, we can look on them with a benign condescension, and pity those still cowering within their doors.

What's wrong with the world?

Sooner or later, every society and every individual has to face up to the question: 'What's wrong with the world?' Nobody believes that the world and the people in it are as perfect as they could possibly be. So a thinking person cannot avoid the issue. What is at the heart of the problem? Our answer to that question will speak volumes about our beliefs and motivations. It will also say a great deal about what we think needs to happen to put right what has gone wrong—what will bring hope, healing, convergence or salvation.

In 1740s Connecticut, the churchgoers packing into the small, wooden churches could have given a clear answer to that question. What's wrong with the world is sin. And the answer is salvation through the blood of Christ. But most people today scarcely have the categories for interpreting these concepts. Like Sanskrit or Cornish, the language of sin and salvation has become, for citizens of a post-Christian culture, a dead language.

In 1973, a leading American psychiatrist called Karl Menninger published a book whose title asked, *Whatever Became of Sin?* (Hodder, 1973). Menninger himself, over his lifetime, had been an eye-witness of the gradual disappearance of sin. He charts the shift from the days when the language of sin was common currency to its gradual erosion in the post-World War II era, and the eclipse of the language of morality by that of psychology. Since Menninger, this shift has continued unabated. For the great majority of today's younger adults and teenagers, talk of sin is rarely more than the stuff of ironic parody. And those who persist in taking the language of sin at face value are generally dismissed as relics of a previous age—irrelevant, bigoted and (most damning of all) uncool.

Today, three main answers are on offer in the developed West to the question of what's wrong with the world. One concentrates on the self: we suffer low self-esteem or self-acceptance. We lack some sort of psychological wholeness in ourselves. This is the answer offered by therapy.

The second focuses around large-scale, global issues such as the destruction of the biosphere, institutional prejudice, or the extinction of animal and plant species. This is the approach taken by most of today's political movements and 'isms': feminism, environmentalism, the gay rights movement, political pressure groups. For such people, what's wrong with the world is something corporate: we live in a society that abuses the environment, denies equal rights to particular groups, where money and power are unevenly distributed, and so on. And so the answer must be a corporate answer: equal rights, the end of patriarchy, a change of government. Salvation entails the death of sexism or heterosexism, ageism, racism, rationalism, consumerism, even speciesism.

The third answer to what's gone wrong with the world is offered by the increasingly popular Eastern and New Age spiritualities, and cults with roots in Eastern mysticism. For these groups, what's wrong is ignorance. The human tragedy is that we lack true consciousness to understand a hidden, mystical truth—such as the illusory nature of the material world, or of our own divinity. This is the approach of Hinduism, Buddhism (including Zen and Tibetan Buddhism), Christian Science, Theosophy, Rosicrucianism, Scientology and Transcendental Meditation. It is the consensus view among Eastern gurus such as Sri Chinmoy, Sai Baba, and many others. It also pervades popular New Age books such as *A Course in Miracles* (Foundation for Inner Peace, 1977) and most new religious groups and seminars with New Age roots.

Notably absent these days is the answer given in 18th-century New England—in fact, the answer given for the whole of Jewish and

Christian history: that the heart of the problem is sin, our individual and corporate failure to be in relationship with God and to live his way; that we are personally guilty, and personally answerable for our failures.

The case against sin

Few people have rejected the traditional Christian diagnosis after a careful weighing of the evidence for and against it. Most people, in any era, shape their beliefs and lifestyles in the context of what sociologists term a 'plausibility structure': what feels likely or plausible to them, because others around them believe it or do it. Certain facts about life and lifestyle will seem self-evidently true to any of us, at any given moment. This seeming truth comes through our family and friends who believe the same things. We see these values reflected back at us on TV and radio, in our magazines, in conversations over a drink in the pub and in the opinion polls we read. The values of the dominant plausibility structure seep in without us realizing it, shaping and reinforcing what we see as 'normal'.

So the reason most people have rejected sin is not for thought-out philosophical, ethical or theological reasons. It is a simple matter of changing fashion. But why has the fashion swung so decisively against sin? And why is it that when thoughtful people do consider the case for believing in sin, plenty reject it as untenable in our own day? There are five main objections levelled against the belief that sin is an accurate diagnosis of what's wrong with the world:

Sin is local

This objection claims that the sheer diversity of beliefs and lifestyles around the world weakens the case for believing in sin. Sin is a purely local idea, and we have no business making greater claims for it than that. This objection takes two slightly different forms.

First, underpinning the traditional idea of sin are some fairly major assumptions. One of these is that there are solid moral obligations 'out there' that people have broken. The preacher who shouts, 'Sinners!' at his congregation is presupposing that there is a standard of morality which is binding on all people, everywhere. He assumes that his hearers share in a real moral guilt, and not that they are simply at odds with a local convention, or that they are lacking in a more subjective attribute such as self-acceptance.

But this assumption, surely, can hardly stand up to close scrutiny. This kind of moralizing was all very well in an earlier day when people's lives were bounded by the perimeter of their own little village and local custom took on the appearance of ethical absolutes. But today we live in a global community, where we can see first-hand the astonishing diversity of cultures and moralities from around the world. So if a particular culture has developed a different morality from ours, who are we to criticize what works for them? Is it not an act of gross insensitivity and intolerance, and even cultural imperialism, to insist that our system of morals applies to all people, everywhere?

This argument, in effect, deconstructs the preacher's entire appeal. When he shouts out, 'Sinners!' all he can possibly mean is, 'You who don't live up to the values of your particular culture!' In a world where values vary from culture to culture, the absolutism of an appeal to sin is inappropriate. The foundations underpinning sin, then, appear to be purely local, easily dissolved when a jugful of corrosive cultural relativism is poured over them.

The second variation on the argument that sin is relative to a particular locality seems equally damning. Not only is the idea of moral obligations underlying sin culturally relative, so too is the idea of sin itself. The briefest skim through any encyclopedia of world religions shows that although all faiths propose an answer to the question 'What's wrong with the world?' the answer they give is not necessarily sin. In fact, many offer an entirely different diagnosis, particularly great Eastern faiths such as Buddhism and Hinduism.

Likewise, many religious traditions native to the West reject the sin diagnosis. Native American spirituality has no emphasis on personal sin. Today's paganism and its close cousin Wicca (witchcraft) explicitly deny sin, as do the New Age spiritualities of writers such as Shirley Maclaine, Carlos Castaneda and Deepak Chopra. How, then, can Christians sustain their claim that sin is a universally valid diagnosis of the human condition, when it is clearly just one option among many in the global supermarket of spiritualities, a purely local belief-system?

Sin is judgmental

This objection is similar to the objection that sin is local, but pushes it further. Not only is it the case that different cultures have different moral codes, say the sceptics. Every single person does too. In the absence of solid, universal codes of ethics that are binding on all people, all I can really know is what works best for *me*. And that will depend on a range of variables: my culture, personality, upbringing, the climate I live in, and so on. What matters is not that I am chained to some law-code, which may have originated in another culture, but that I am true to myself. In the words of singer Geri Halliwell, 'Everybody's truth is different'.

It follows, then, that if these sceptics are right, I have no right to criticize others. In fact, if I claim that another person's actions are sinful, all I am doing in reality is trying to gain some sort of power over them, to coerce them to behave in ways I want them to behave, rather than leaving them free to be themselves. All moral codes are power games, claim the sceptics. Not only is it wrong to call another person a sinner, it is actually wrong to make any moral judgments at all about another person.

Sin is outdated

These first two objections localize the idea of sin in terms of *place*. The first reduces the area where moral obligations apply (and consequently, where criticism of breaking them applies) to one particular culture, and the second reduces it further, to an individual person. This third objection localizes sin in *time*. We live today in a rapidly changing culture, which takes for granted a bewildering range of innovations unthinkable to earlier generations: developments in technology, communications, transport, and so on. We have access to a vaster range of knowledge and cultural data than any society in history.

Now think about the idea of sin, say the sceptics. Its roots supposedly lie in a moment of pre-history, or non-historical myth, involving forbidden fruit and a talking snake. It was developed in a primitive agrarian community in the Middle East, quite different from our technologically sophisticated urban culture. It was refined in pre-modern North Africa and had its heyday in medieval Europe and Puritan America. Like it or not, sin is simply an old-fashioned idea, based on premises people today can no longer accept.

Sin is wrong-headed

We saw, in the first of the sceptics' objections, how the traditional understanding of sin has certain vital underpinnings. One of these is the idea that there is such a thing as a universal 'ought', a moral law which the sinner has personally broken. The first three objections questioned the existence or universal validity of this law.

This next objection now shifts the focus to the person supposedly breaking the law. Even if there were some sort of ideals of behaviour that were binding on all people, and even if people fall short of those ideals, does it automatically follow that they are sinners? Are they necessarily choosing to do wrong? Surely not, the sceptics suggest. It could equally be the case (in fact, they say, it is more likely) that people's shortcomings are no fault of their own. People are more victims than villains, more sinned against than sinning. This truth may have been obscured in earlier generations, but a more compassionate age can now recognize it.

A clear example of this is people's own backgrounds and life experience. Many critics of the sin diagnosis argue in the following terms: 'That prostitute on the street corner: some moralists would call her a sinner, but the way she is now is largely the product of abuse she suffered in childhood. And that woman who stabbed her husband when he lay drunk in bed: who can blame her, after all the violence she suffered at his hands? Or that man who was caught shoplifting: he is surely a victim of poverty and social injustice, more deserving of our compassion than our blame. It seems an inaccurate and cruel diagnosis to accuse people of sin, and call on them to repent of that sin—when they are more accurately described as victims of life and society.'

Another area where many critics claim that people are more victims than villains is addiction. Addiction removes from individuals the power to choose. The drug addict who steals to fund his habit is a victim. It is, in effect, the drugs that are doing the stealing. The alcoholic who strikes out at his partner is the victim of the alcohol in his system: it is the bottle which hits out. Four out of every five serious assaults in the UK are alcohol-related. In each case, the addict or drinker seems more victim than culprit. Again, the remedy ought to be compassionate help with the addiction, rather than punishment or blame.

Sin is morbid

This objection concerns the general atmosphere generated by talk of sin. Like our first objection, it has two main points to it.

First, people who go on about sin have some sort of problem with pleasure. They are stern moralists who are out to stop other people having a good time. This is why sin figured so prominently in the theology of the Puritans. Sin-mongers are morbid people, who hate to see others enjoying themselves—especially where drink, music and sex are concerned.

Second, people in any case are really not as bad as all that. To listen to people who believe in sin, you might think people are all as bad as they could possibly be. Christian moralists always assume the worst about human nature. This must stem from an almost pathologically morbid state of mind, the sort of mind that refuses to see things the way they are, but is always looking to stir up guilt, shame and self-disgust. The world is actually a rather nice place, and people are basically nice too.

Jonathan Edwards in the shopping mall

Sin, then, stands in the dock condemned by the critics for being local, judgmental, outdated, wrong-headed and morbid. Let's put all this another way. Imagine the 18th-century preacher Jonathan Edwards standing up in a seating area inside a modern-day shopping mall. Justin, 26, takes a break from his shopping to listen. His first reaction is amusement: 'ranting nutter'. His second reaction is bafflement: 'where does this guy get all these weird ideas from?' His third reaction is outrage: 'how dare he speak to me like that—and in that tone of voice?' These are all gut reactions.

But after a few moments, Justin realizes that a gut reaction is hardly an adequate basis for rejecting somebody's views. So he tries to unravel the main strands that make up his objection to the man's message and manner.

1 This guy is telling me I'm a sinner. But all he really means is that whatever culture he comes from happens not to approve of a particular thing I do. If he was from Mongolia or New Guinea, of course he'd have a different set of values. Judging by his accent, he happens to come from America—a culture where lots of people believe that the thing messing up the world is sin. But that idea wasn't a part of my upbringing. So it doesn't apply to me anyway.

2 Not only that. Even if we were from the same culture, how could he know what's right and wrong for me? All he can ever know is what's right for him. So what he's really trying to do is to trick me in some way. He's using these emotional speeches to lure me into his control. Probably wants to make me join his group and become an oddball like him.

3 What he's saying is old-fashioned, and irrelevant to today's world.

4 In any case, it's unfair and cruel to call people sinners. In life, you play the hand they deal you, and some people just get dealt a bad hand. You can hardly blame people for living messed-up lives, if circumstances or other people have conspired to mess things up for them.

5 He's clearly a miserable old so-and-so, who wants to stop other people enjoying themselves, and who likes the idea of lowering people's self-esteem. In reality, people aren't nearly as bad as he makes out.

Enter the Christian critics

These five objections to believing in sin are so prevalent in Western society that they have become truisms: most people simply take them for granted. They form a part of the dominant 'plausibility structure', particularly among young adults, and together they appear to make up a compelling case.

It might be expected that the Christian Church's response to this scepticism would be to redouble its efforts in explaining and defending the doctrine of sin. Sure enough, in some circles this certainly has been the case. In other church circles, however, some serious questions are being asked about just how relevant the church's traditional emphasis on sin really has been. Some of those taking a pickaxe to the foundations of sin are the very custodians of Christian doctrine who might be most expected to defend it from others' attacks. For the sake of accuracy and completeness we need, then, to add another set of objections, those of the Christian critics.

Christians who question the church's traditional focus on sin claim that, far from helping the cause of faith, sin might actually act as an obstacle to it. They offer a number of specific challenges.

It is unbiblical

Around the year 400, a British monk called Pelagius settled in Rome, where he developed a theology that challenged the church's traditional emphasis on sin. He utterly rejected the idea that we all inherit a bias towards wrongdoing, or that people's capacity for self-improvement is severely limited by sin. For Pelagius, people are born sinless—and may continue to lead a sinless life. In this scenario, God's role is not to rescue the helpless, or provide some kind of atoning sacrifice to remove sin. It is simply to provide good laws to live by, and the good moral example of Jesus Christ. The Bible, then, becomes less a story of fall and rescue than God's way of helping us achieve our own unlimited potential. According to Pelagius, lots of biblical characters did remain sinless.

Pelagius was the first major spokesman for a view which has recurred throughout church history. It is the claim that sin-obsessed Christians have simply misread the Bible by looking at it through bifocal lenses of sin and salvation and that, rightly understood, the faith is more optimistic about human nature.

In the 19th century, the emerging Liberal theology of the day rediscovered this image of Jesus as a role model and teacher of human potential. In Germany, the theologian Adolf von Harnack (1851–1930) put forward the view (resurrected recently by the English novelist A.N. Wilson, among many others) that the true message of Jesus was a simple message about the universal fatherhood of God, leading to a simple ethical challenge about the brotherhood of man. This, he claimed, had then been distorted by the early Church—especially the apostle Paul, who transformed it into our dogmas about the incarnation of the Son of God and blood shed in atonement for sin.

In 1963, the radical English theologian John Robinson published his controversial book *Honest to God* (SCM Press), in which he described the Christian idea of Jesus Christ dying for sin as 'frankly incredible to man come of age', claiming that humanity's only real problem is our lack of love. Meanwhile in America, a Reformed Church of America pastor called Norman Vincent Peale was putting a different spin on a similar message. Peale's best-known work was the international bestseller, *The Power of Positive Thinking* (Prentice-Hall, 1952). Peale's 'possibility thinking' re-defines evil as anything which holds us back from achieving our full potential. Sin is a lack of self-confidence, leading to unhappiness and lack of success. For Peale, human nature is infinitely perfectible. All you need is the right attitude.

Peale's emphasis recurs in the teachings of Robert Schuller of the Crystal Cathedral—at the time of writing, the only major US televangelist who is not either evangelical, fundamentalist or Pentecostal in his theology. Much of Schuller's teaching is fairly mainstream, but his teaching on sin shows a clear debt to Peale. His book *Self-Esteem: The New Reformation* (Word, 1982) claims that the Protestant Reformers of the 16th century had a defective understanding of human psychology. Had they better understood the Bible and human nature, he claims, they would have seen that sin is not so much rebellion against God, but more a lack of self-worth. In this scenario, at the heart of salvation lies a more positive assessment of the self, attained through personal success and achievement, with God's help.

Similarly, the movement known as Creation Spirituality also

questions the dominant Christian emphasis on sin and redemption. Its best-known representative is Matthew Fox, an independent-minded Dominican-turned-Anglican priest and author. In *Original Blessing* (Bear & Co, 1983), Fox bitterly attacks historic Christianity for finding its central motifs in sin and salvation. He claims that this emphasis on sin not only distorts the person and message of Jesus (p. 20), it has led to most of the problems of Western Christianity and society. The real villain of the piece, for Matthew Fox, is Augustine of Hippo (354–430), whose theology firmly emphasized fall and redemption. Augustine's theology was, says Fox, 'abysmal' and 'one-sided' (p. 22).

Instead, Fox points to God's original act of creation as a more positive focus for spirituality. We should be not so much looking for salvation from a damaged human nature as learning to befriend and celebrate ourselves and God's good creation. For Matthew Fox, if there is any kind of 'original sin' at all, it is the fact that many people still cling to an outmoded fall–redemption way of looking at the world! It is significant that many people influenced by Creation Spirituality have been calling in recent years for the church to rehabilitate Pelagius as a prophet, rather than to perpetuate the traditional view of him as a heretic. At the end of *Original Blessing*, Matthew Fox lists a catalogue of writers and mystics who he believes are fellow travellers in the quest for a creation-centred spirituality. These include New Agers, Wiccans and representatives of non-Christian religions such as Taoism and Zen Buddhism. Clearly, if Fox is on target in all his criticisms, a major rethink of what Christians believe and how they relate to other spiritual traditions is long overdue.

Varieties of Pelagianism, then, have long been minority options around the fringes of Christianity. But in the post-Christian climate of today's West, where the language of sin is falling into disuse, a growing number of Christians of different traditions are exploring whether a spirituality no longer based around sin and guilt might be a creative, more appealing way forward than historic orthodoxy.

A wrong emphasis

This second challenge is less radical than the Pelagian, Liberal and Creation Spirituality challenges. It is a charge levelled by some Pentecostal and charismatic Christians, whose beliefs include the mainstream Christian view that what's wrong with the world is sin, and that Jesus Christ came to die for the sins of the world. This particular Pentecostal challenge is more about where emphasis is placed within the historic faith.

In this Pentecostal model, the great climax of the biblical story is the coming of the Holy Spirit on Jesus' disciples on the Day of Pentecost. That is the moment when the Church was born, the Spirit was made available to all believers, and the supernatural gifts of God were released. The death and resurrection of Jesus are, of course, vital precursors to the coming of the Spirit, but we should not linger on Good Friday, or even Easter Sunday—we should fast-forward to Pentecost. It is the coming of the Spirit that impacts the Church today. It is the power of the Spirit that draws people to God, and which we can experience today in worship and acts of power.

Some charismatic-leaning churches inside mainstream denominations may not express things quite so bluntly—that Pentecost supersedes Easter. But the fact remains that in many churches the high point of the worship, the moment for which the congregation waits with bated breath, is the time when chairs are cleared aside and a 'time of ministry' begins. This involves inviting the Holy Spirit to come in power, and an expectation of physical signs such as shaking uncontrollably, weeping, tingling hands, collapsing 'in the Spirit' and receiving 'words of knowledge' from God. In such services, whatever the creed in the official service book may say, the clear emphasis is less on the death of Christ for sins than on the coming of the Spirit in power.

Jonathan Edwards saw similarly strong physical reactions in congregations during the Great Awakening in New England. But there was an important difference. In Enfield, Connecticut, people's violent physical reactions were responses to an overwhelming sense of their own sin, and their wonder at the atoning death of Christ. In many contemporary Pentecostal and charismatic services, people expect to be overwhelmed principally by the power of the Spirit. Such Pentecostals find a focus on sin and salvation necessary as a station to pass through, but hardly a terminus. The coming of the promised Spirit at Pentecost, and the implications of this momentous event for the Church, are where the real action is.

A wrong picture of God

Like the previous challenge, this one is less radical than the first—that the idea of sin is actually unbiblical. But it is a potent challenge none the less. It claims that the traditional doctrine of sin is not so much wrong as only one part of the picture and, if seen in isolation, will produce a distorted picture both of God and the Christian life. Its main advocates are a large number of recent Evangelical writers, who describe them- selves as 'post-conservative' or 'open' in their theology.

Perhaps the best expression of this challenge comes in the book *Unbounded Love* (IVP, 1994), by Canadian theologians Clark Pinnock and Robert Brow. In it, they point out that the traditional focus on sin assumes a certain backdrop, and a certain image of who God is. The backdrop is a courtroom, and the image of God is primarily as a judge, motivated by wrath.

By contrast, Pinnock and Brow insist that in the Bible the backdrop to the whole drama is a family relationship. And they say that the main image of God is as a Father or lover, whose characteristic emotion is not wrath, but compassion. The drama of sin and salvation, in other words, is played out in a relational framework, not a legal one. The contrast with Jonathan Edwards is clear—despite the fact that Pinnock and Brow, like Edwards, operate within the parameters of historic Christianity. For Edwards, the sinful human being is a 'spider or some loathsome insect', held 'over the fire' by an angry God. For Pinnock and Brow, the sinful human being is a prodigal son, whose father waits patiently at the window for his return. This contrast carries theological weight and emotional force. It is not hard to appreciate why the older wrath-and-judgment view is losing favour, even among some trad- itional Christians.

Hindering outreach

In the early 18th century, an English aristocrat called Selina, Countess of Huntingdon, heard the preaching of Methodist pioneer George

Whitefield and converted to the Christian faith. She then set about contacting all her aristocratic friends to invite them to hear Whitefield too. One of the people she contacted was her friend, the Duchess of Buckingham. In her reply, the Duchess commented on the message that George Whitefield was preaching:

It is monstrous to be told that you have a heart as sinful as the common wretches that crawl on the earth. This is highly offensive and insulting; and I cannot but wonder that your ladyship should relish any sentiments so much at variance with high rank and good breeding.

For the Duchess, Whitefield's focus on sin was ill-judged and personally offensive. Far from attracting her to the preacher, it was a turn-off. If this was true in the 18th century, how much more true must this be in our own day, when the great majority not only find talk of sin offensive, they find it outdated and irrelevant.

In the streets of London I regularly come across street evangelists, eager to share their faith with passers-by. Convinced that before people can hear the good news they first need to understand the bad news, they stand waving large black Bibles and yelling about sin. Most of these evangelists come across, frankly, as weird and unhinged. They induce in the passer-by not so much conviction of sin and a need for salvation as mild amusement, or discomfort and embarrassment.

It is hard not to sympathize more with the passers-by than with the evangelist. For most people today, the language of sin is a dead language. Simply shouting that language even louder hardly seems calculated to evoke a sympathetic response. A focus on sin, then, seems, on the face of it, likely to hinder outreach. Consequently, few Christians today appeal mainly to a sense of sin when sharing their faith with others. Sin is simply not a felt need for most people.

Maybe things were different in previous eras. We know that many first-century Jewish believers were wrestling with questions of how they could live in a covenant relationship with a holy God, and erase the obstacle of sin. This was also a live issue at the time of the 16th-century Reformation in Europe, and the 18th-century Awakening in North

America. If so, an evangelistic appeal which presented Christ as the answer to the sin problem came as good news. These days, claim the Christian critics, it surely makes little sense to present Jesus as the answer to a question nobody is asking.

Excessive individualism

Tirades against human sin have historically tended to focus on particular actions committed by an individual person, say the critics. And this focus is not just a recent product of our own individualistic Western culture. The idea of seven 'deadly sins' emerged in the early monasteries of the Eastern Church during the fourth century. The list was officially codified under Pope Gregory the Great (590–604), as pride, envy, anger, sloth, avarice, gluttony and lust. Pope Gregory claimed that these seven encapsulated 'the normal perils of the soul in the ordinary conditions of life'.

In other words, these seven deadly sins were deemed to be the main obstacles blocking the path of an individual wanting to live a holy life. For most of Christian history the first of these, pride, was singled out as being the essence of individual sin. In the 17th century, many identified the fatal sin as gluttony, and saw the Great Fire of London in 1666 as a punishment for the capital's greed (fuelled by the fact that the fire had begun in Pudding Lane and ended at Pie Corner!). During the Victorian era, moralists tended to point their big guns at the last sin on the list— lust. We still live with the legacy of this emphasis. If the word 'sin' evokes anything these days, it is likely to be solitary sexual fantasy, or inappropriate sexual encounter.

But whether the sin *du jour* was pride, lust, sloth or whatever, one thing has remained more or less constant. Sin has been seen in terms of individual temptation, individual wrongdoing and individual guilt. What place for a traditional understanding of sin in our society, whose concern has shifted to wider issues than individual guilt? This might include global dilemmas (extinction of species, international debt, patriarchy), or corporate malpractice (corrupt political structures or company ethos, institutional racism) which no individual can possibly control. None of these massive and widespread wrongs can be laid at the door of any single person. Nor does it seem appropriate for any individual to bear the weight of them on her own shoulders. The language of sin is not only a dead language, it appears, but one too inflexible to cope with the conditions and insights of a new and changing era. So claim the critics.

The strength of the case against sin

The case against sin, then, seems solid and irrefutable. Granted, most people in our own culture have turned against it unthinkingly, as fashions have changed, and without really thinking it through. But it appears that when we do hold the doctrine of sin under the microscope many find it to be local, judgmental, outdated, wrong-headed, and morbid. Added to this, many Christians, supposedly the defenders of the Church's historic doctrines, see it as a major obstacle. Specifically, sin stands accused of being unbiblical, putting the theological emphasis in the wrong place, giving a wrong picture of God, hindering outreach and being over-individualistic.

Has the day finally come when we ought to switch off the life-support machine and give this ailing doctrine a decent burial? Or are we missing something? In the next chapter we shall examine more closely the arguments of the secular sceptics outlined earlier in this chapter. We shall look to see whether the foundations of the sceptical stance are themselves any more durable. Then, in Chapter 3, we shall tackle each of the specifically Christian objections we have just considered. In both chapters, we may be in for a few surprises.

CHAPTER 2

Sceptical about the Secular Sceptics

Thinking is what a great many people think they are doing when they are merely rearranging their prejudices.

WILLIAM JAMES, PHILOSOPHER

Whoever marries the spirit of this age will find himself a widower in the next.

WILLIAM RALPH INGE, DEAN OF ST PAUL'S

Thinking for ourselves

In Chapter 1 we encountered the main arguments against the Christian idea of sin. First, the secular sceptics picture the doctrine of sin as something resembling an ancient house. This old house, they say, is based on shaky foundations (the idea that there are universal moral obligations, binding on all people, which we all break). Not only that: this house built on weak foundations is itself unsound. Sin, claim the sceptics, is an outdated, inaccurate diagnosis, perpetuated by morbid religious types.

The second set of arguments, from certain Christian critics, finds the idea of sin to be an obstacle in working out a relevant spirituality for our times. We shall return to these Christian critics in the next chapter. For now, we are concerned with weighing up the charges levelled by the secular sceptics. Specifically, we shall carry out a surveyor's report on the foundations the sin-residence is built on, and then ask whether the critics' own house might, in fact, be less sturdy than the one they are criticizing.

Just one word of warning as we begin this chapter. As we proceed, we shall need to do something most people today rarely do. We shall question many of the fashionable opinions of our own day, even those that seem self-evidently true because we have heard them so often—in school, in the workplace, in the media and in the pub. We shall, in other words, be doing something risky and subversive: thinking for ourselves.

Is sin really local?

The first piece of foundation the secular sceptics find to be weak is this: that sin is too local to be true. They rightly point out that the idea of sin assumes universal, moral obligations 'out there' which apply to all people, and which people have broken. Against this, the sceptic counters that all we can really know is a morality that works for our own culture. Who are we, they ask, to criticize anybody else's culture, and what works for that culture—even if it is based on a very different value system from our own? To judge other people's systems of values seems both arrogant and intolerant.

This is an argument from *cultural relativism*, the belief that moral values are a product of human cultures, and only really apply within a particular culture. All that matters, for the cultural relativist, is that a given society agrees on a certain set of values, and that these are then passed on to its children. But we must look more closely at the foundations that this case is built on. Cultural relativism, for all its current popularity, has some major cracks in its own underpinnings.

One crack is that the evidence seems to be against it, if we compare the actual value systems of different human cultures. If cultural relativism were true, we might expect to see a whole range of moralities around the world—each coherent within themselves, but quite different (or even slightly different) from the others. In fact, the heart of human moral codes—around the world and through the ages—remains stubbornly and boringly similar. In an appendix to his powerful little book *The Abolition of Man* (OUP, 1943), C.S. Lewis assembles a long list of moral precepts from cultures across the ancient world, vastly separated by time and geography—from the ancient Norsemen to indigenous Australians, via ancient Egypt. Time after time, identical values recur: do not murder, love your neighbour, respect your parents, do not commit adultery, be honest, seek justice, do not lie, show mercy.

These are, of course, the same moral obligations that we find in the biblical Ten Commandments and that you and I feel today. And this is one of the big flaws in cultural relativism. The evidence of actual cultures points to a startling fact: that people everywhere seem aware of the same set of basic moral obligations. The cultural relativist, then, has to exaggerate relatively minor differences, usually to do with dress or sexual customs, to support his case.

But on closer inspection, even these apparent differences can hardly be said to stem from genuinely different value systems. Often, they simply arise from differences in climate or fashion. All cultures and sub-cultures, for example, have taboos about modesty in dress. But how such taboos are expressed will vary dramatically from Lapland to Mali, from the Plymouth Brethren to the heavy metal sub-culture. The underlying principle is the same, but how different groups of people apply it will vary.

But cultural relativism has an even bigger flaw than the underlying moral similarities between cultures. If cultural relativism is true, nobody has any basis for criticizing any other culture. If there is no other standard than whatever a certain culture happens to agree on, critics can only say resignedly, 'Well, we might not like it, but it must be OK for them.' But let's pursue this thought for a moment. Isn't it within the realms of possibility that leaders in another culture might agree on a particular course of action which we find deeply, absolutely *wrong*, even *evil*? Consider Nazi Germany—or Amin's Uganda, Pol Pot's Cambodia, or Stalin's Russia. In reality, we still find ourselves shaken to the core as we read of the evils carried out under these regimes, and we should expect any right-thinking person to feel the same way.

In 1933, over 17 million Germans voted for the Nazi Party. This represented more than 44 per cent of the German population. The Party's vision of a powerful, racially pure Fatherland commanded widespread support. But did that make it morally right?

The moment we begin to question the actions of Hitler and his Nazis, and the support they received from large sections of the German people, we are flatly denying cultural relativism. We can only say the actions of

Hitler were wrong, immoral or evil by appealing to a standard of morality which is bigger than Hitler, the German people, and ourselves. And if we suggest that a given country has 'improved' or 'progressed' in terms of its policies and actions (that Cambodia, for example, has improved since the departure of the bloody Khmer Rouge regime), we are again denying cultural relativism. If morality really is relative, from time to time and from place to place, nobody can ever judge any practices in another culture.

During the post-World War II Nuremberg trials, Nazi war criminals defended themselves by claiming that what they did was acceptable within the value system of Nazi Germany, and that people standing outside that system had no right to criticize it. Their argument, in other words, was based on the pure cultural relativism which had motivated Nazi ideology from the start. Nazism was deeply rooted in a conviction that there are no universal or binding human laws or values. What motivated Hitler and his cronies was a vaguely and personally defined 'good of the Fatherland'. This conviction was used to justify all kinds of atrocities, and eliminate any number of people deemed to be enemies of the state. This is the morality of the tyrant and the thug. It is no coincidence that the Nazis were deeply and resolutely opposed to the Christian concept of sin.

The whole Nazi way of arguing was decisively rejected by the judges at Nuremberg, and rightly so. Accepting it would have sent out a clear message: that any practice, from racism to infanticide, becomes acceptable if it gains widespread support in a particular culture. In today's world we have internationally accepted standards of law, conventions on human rights and cross-border police forces. For these to have any credibility and effectiveness, we have to take one big thing for granted: that the moral and legal codes of different cultures are not so fundamentally different after all.

This flaw in cultural relativism becomes particularly clear if we turn the whole question round, and ask whether a person from another culture has any right to question the morality of the culture we live in. The answer, of course, is that they have every right to challenge aspects of what we do. In fact, their distance is a positive asset. They are able to see us with a level of clarity and detachment that we can't manage because we are so immersed in our own culture. This is, of course, why so many Westerners pay attention to the likes of Gandhi, Solzhenitsyn and the Dalai Lama, and groups such as the native Americans and Australians, when they criticize our shallow consumerism.

However, if we allow ourselves to be challenged by wisdom from abroad, and if we start to agree with what a friendly, insightful critic says, we undermine cultural relativism. If cultures really are relative, these critics should hold their tongues. We should be laughing off their insights as irrelevant outside their own little world. In a culturally relative world, their only business would be their own culture.

There is a third big flaw in cultural relativism, besides the fact that basic values seem to be universal, and our innate sense that people have a right to speak out when they see wrong done, whether in their own culture or another. It is this: what if people within a given culture disagree with each other? It is all very well to speak of other cultures as if all people in them had the same values. In fact, no culture is monolithic in this way.

The caste system in India goes back millennia, with deep roots in Hindu religion and Indian culture. Equally, plenty of Indians today judge the caste system to be unjust and offensive. How should we, as outsiders, view the caste system? A pure cultural relativist might want to say, 'Caste is part of traditional Indian culture, so I respect that.' But to say that is to deny the insights of the many Indians who want to abolish the caste system. Which 'culture within a culture' should the cultural relativist respect?

This applies to every controversial moral issue that is debated within a given culture. It also applies to political and religious regimes: should we always respect a country's right to enforce religious or cultural laws on its citizens, or can we support its dissidents? The cultural relativist simply has no basis for applauding any reform movements, or for making value judgments between conflicting views within a culture. Whatever has been, must be right. Cultural relativism, then, is profoundly reactionary, disturbingly immoral and deeply antagonistic to human rights. It is so deeply flawed as to be untenable.

Is sin really judgmental?

But wait. Maybe the problem with cultural relativism is that it is not radical enough. Maybe we need to abandon the untenable halfway house of a morality that applies inside one particular culture, but not outside it. This more radical step is to conclude that every single individual simply has to find a morality that works for them—Geri Halliwell's 'Everybody's truth is different'.

That brings us to the second argument of the sceptics: that all I can know is what works for me personally, and that we need to abandon any pretence that values are shared—either universally, or within a given culture. This is a position known as *individual relativism*, or *subjectivism*. It goes hand-in-hand with *emotivism*, which claims that when a person expresses a moral opinion over an action, this opinion says nothing about the action itself. In this scenario, a moral stance cannot possibly be 'true' or 'false', since there is no objective measuring stick to measure it against. All this person is doing is expressing their own emotions, how they personally feel about a course of action. Values become a statement of personal taste. For the individual relativist, the whole idea of sin is terribly judgmental. Who has the right to judge what another person can feel about life? In fact, for the individual relativist, all moral judgments about other people are suspect. The only person whose actions I can speak about with any authority, says the individual relativist, is myself.

How firm are the foundations of this view of morals? The first point to note is that *individual* relativism is quite incompatible with *cultural* relativism. Justin in the shopping mall, the sceptical voice on page 20, slipped from one to the other, as if both were self-evidently true. First he claimed that a code of values is valid within a given culture, but not outside it. He said, about the preacher whose words so infuriated him, 'All he really means is that whatever culture he comes from happens not to approve of a particular thing I do.' Next he said, 'Even if we were from the same culture, how could he know what's right and wrong for me?' In fact, these two statements are not only far from self-evident; they simply cannot both be true at the same time. The first assumes a framework of *cultural* relativism, claiming that a moral code is binding on everybody in a given culture. The second, on the other hand, assumes a framework of *individual* relativism, claiming that no moral code is binding on anybody except the one which the individual personally accepts. So Justin's own reactions were internally inconsistent. Individual relativism undermines cultural relativism. But is it an improvement on it?

Individual relativism sounds consistent in theory. It certainly avoids pitfalls of the cultural relativist, such as the fact that people within cultures do not always agree with each other. However, it is hard to live out in practice. If my home is burgled, I believe that what the burglar did is wrong. If my best friend is murdered in a drive-by shooting, that is wrong too. But the consistent individual relativist has problems explaining why these actions are wrong. In fact, given his framework of values, they are not wrong at all. The burglar whose personal moral code includes stealing from the homes of the wealthy (or the not-so-wealthy), or the street gangster whose moral code includes eliminating rivals, is simply being consistent with his own value system.

If a man punches me in the face as I walk down the street, I do not accept his explanation that he felt it was the right thing to do at that moment. I expect him and other passers-by to know that what he did was wrong, and I expect the legal system to agree with me. In fact, in daily life, when we come across people whose only value is what they feel to be right for them, and act accordingly, we do not approvingly call them individual relativists. We call them criminally insane, or say they have other mental health problems. Why? Because we expect everybody to accept the same set of basic moral obligations that we accept. We expect everybody to have a conscience that relates in some way to an inbuilt, universal, common-sense code of values. And we rightly imprison or hospitalize those who cannot see this, and who act as if values are simply a matter of personal taste, because they pose a serious threat to others.

From the earliest years, children exclaim, 'That's not fair!' They soon recognize that cheating and lying are wrong, that hurting others is wrong. If they sometimes seem not to live this out with regard to others, they certainly recognize the wrongness of it when they are the ones who are cheated, lied to or hurt! We all live as if there really are moral obligations on us, as if moral standards are there to be recognized rather than invented. Our sense of morality is not something trivial and easily changed: it is deeply rooted in what it is to be human, and in the ways we live together in community. To believe in sin as wrongdoing, then, is not judgmental. It simply follows from the common-sense idea that some things are right and some things are wrong. The alternative to believing in right and wrong is too appalling to contemplate. To confront the child abuser or the cheat is not judgmental, it is an act of justice and compassion—both for the victims and the perpetrator.

We can put all this another way. The individual relativist claims that there are no moral obligations that are binding on everybody. From here, he concludes that the idea of sin is judgmental. But his own statement ('believing in sin is judgmental') is itself a strongly held and clearly expressed moral value-judgment. He is singling out one aspect of traditional morality (the worthwhile idea that we should respect others' basic freedom to discover their own uniqueness, and to express themselves freely) and he is making it the supreme value that trumps all others.

In other words, all arguments against moral judgments are themselves based on moral judgments. They have to be, by definition. The position of the individual relativist in practice self-destructs, because he is himself doing what he has ruled off-limits. He is making a moral statement which he believes is absolutely true for all people. As in the last chapter, a vital distinction has to be drawn here between an attitude of *judgmentalism*—which is insensitive, heavy-handed moralizing—and making moral *judgments*—which is good and necessary for any person or society that believes in good and evil, or right and wrong. Not only is it possible to reject one and keep the other—it is essential.

So where has individual relativism come from? It is clearly the product of an individualistic consumer culture, which has attempted to extend its hallowed ideal of absolute, unfettered personal freedom into every area of life—even those areas where it has no business to be. To those of us living in a culture of hyperchoice, such relativism feels plausible and carries a warm glow of tolerance. But on closer inspection its foundations are seen to be riven with cracks. It is a fashion of thought that only seems so attractive because it happens to be a current fad.

In practice, individual relativism is also vulnerable to most of the criticisms we levelled at cultural relativism. It cannot account for the basic similarities in moral codes from around the world, throughout history. It gives no basis for questioning whatever another culture decides to do, such as the Khmer Rouge or Nazi regimes. It actually makes the problem worse. It not only supports the right of pre-war Germany to choose the Nazis, it allows every individual Nazi to do whatever he personally feels is right. It gives no basis for other cultures to question our practices. In fact, it makes things worse, by claiming that even other individuals close to me have no basis for questioning whatever I choose to do. It is a disaster.

Here, we need a brief digression to respond to a possible objection. Somebody might object in the following terms: 'Listen. In practice, nobody actually lives up to the values of traditional morality. We all do things wrong from time to time. Doesn't that mean that traditional values are unworkable? We might as well forget traditional morality, if nobody consistently keeps it anyway!' But this is a misunderstanding. There is all the difference in the world between, on the one hand, denying that there are moral obligations binding on all people and, on the other hand, accepting this but failing to live up to these obligations all the time.

The individual relativist says there is no 'ought' that should influence his lifestyle decisions. To which we reply: sorry, but we all experience just such an 'ought' every day of our lives, even if we sometimes fall short of its demands. It is the difference between knowing I must love and be faithful to my wife, even though I sometimes don't spend as much time with her as I should and sometimes find myself looking appreciatively at other women, and denying that my marriage vows are in any way binding on my lifestyle choices at all. There is all the difference in the world.

At the end of the day, individual relativism is simply wrong-headed. It assumes that values are always open to being reinvented, that they are a purely individual construct. In fact, every person's sense of morality is more like the air they breathe, or the ground they walk on. It is so fundamental to our human make-up that we cannot even challenge an aspect of traditional morality without assuming another part of that same morality as the basis of our criticism. To try to stand outside our inherited core of universal moral obligation is like trying to stand outside language, or the atmosphere.

Some will point out that equally sincere people come to differing conclusions on difficult moral issues such as abortion. This is true, of course. But see what is happening here. Both sides in the abortion debate appeal to fundamental moral principles such as sanctity of life and human rights. One side applies these same principles primarily to the unborn child; the other side, to the mother (arguing that the child is still in some sense a 'potential life', which should not be prioritized at the expense of the mother). Neither side argues that sanctity of life and human dignity are in themselves wrong principles: the debate is over how best to apply our fundamental moral obligations in a messy, real-life situation.

Each one of us has a deeply rooted, built-in core of moral obligations that seem self-evidently right. And this core of morality appears to be one we share with our family, community and society, and with those of other cultures. But the consistent relativist has to deny the obvious. He has to say that even our most fundamental moral impulses really are up for grabs, and that different cultures or individuals could create new ones as they choose.

Individual relativism is not only wrong-headed, it is unlivable. A consistent individual relativist would either be an evil criminal who was a danger to society, or a person caught up in their own sad little universe, denying all that makes shared life and communication possible. Individual relativism also plays directly into the hands of thugs, racists and bigots, by undercutting the moral values by which we can condemn such people's actions. There are huge flaws in individual relativism. We put our faith in it at our own peril. It is doubtful how long our society, and our own sanity, can remain sound if we do.

One of my favourite stories from the local newspaper in my former parish, the *Hackney Gazette*, was their report on the annual Anarchists'

Five-a-Side Football Tournament. Every year the local anarchist community celebrates Hackney Anarchy Week, and the centrepiece of the
week is a grand picnic in the park and a football tournament. The idea
of anarchist football might seem a contradiction in terms. Anarchy
means the absence of order or rules, and comes from the Greek
anarchos, 'without a ruler'. Sure enough, during the football matches,
according to the *Gazette* report, 'anarchy prevailed'.

The matches all came to a great climax with the goalposts being
symbolically ripped down, by way of protest against external authorities
dictating to the anarchists where they ought to be kicking, or drawing
oppressive distinctions between real goals and missed goals. Far better,
thought the Hackney Anarchists, to rip down the goals altogether so
that everybody could do their own thing. Individual relativism, pushed
to its logical conclusion, means you can't even stage something as
simple as a football match. It makes an even worse basis for life and
morals.

Many people today are so afraid of being judgmental that they feel
paralysed from making any kind of moral judgments. But the two are
not the same thing at all. To be judgmental is to be somebody who
constantly points out the failures of others and adopts a tone of moral
superiority. We rightly want to avoid becoming self-righteous prigs. But
making moral judgments is quite different. It is about concern for our
families, friends and neighbourhoods, about protecting children and
other vulnerable people, about punishing cruelty and injustice. Moral
judgments are the essential basis for any caring, fair community.

Is sin really outdated?

The third objection from Chapter 1 localized the idea of sin not just in
place, but also in time. It claimed that belief in sin has become
untenable in our rapidly changing culture, with our bewildering pace of
technical innovation. But a moment's inspection will reveal the cracks
in this sceptical foundation too.

This argument claims that the passing of time changes the boundaries of good and evil, right and wrong. But this argument is clearly
bizarre and flawed. If true, it would undercut the basis for bringing

Serbians or Rwandans to justice for crimes committed decades earlier. It would remove our right to criticize anything our own society or any other society did in the past. In fact, the longer ago the action was, the more immune from criticism that society would become. On this basis, Serbian or Rwandan war crimes from the 1990s might be deemed evil; the colonialism and slavery of an earlier era, wrong but understandable; the Crusades and the Inquisition, slightly questionable; the Emperor Diocletian's martyrdom of the early Christians, or child sacrifice in ancient Carthage, quite acceptable. If morals truly change with the times, we have little basis for revulsion or outrage at anything that happened in an earlier era.

Something deep inside us rightly reacts against this kind of relativism through history, just as we react against attempts to relativize good and evil geographically. Something inside us wants to insist that in some fundamental way, good is good and evil is evil, whether in first-century Rome or 21st-century London.

Is sin really wrong-headed?

This argument claims that whether or not we believe in morality as relative, local or universal, it is always unfair to blame people for the wrongs they do. People are victims more than villains.

It is true that much Christian theology and popular preaching has tended to portray humanity in the worst possible light, as villains (remember Jonathan Edwards' 'loathsome insects'). It is equally true that our post-Freudian society now portrays people as victims of forces beyond their control: parents, society, poverty, addictions, and so on. Overeaters are less likely to be seen as gluttonous Billy Bunters than as 'food addicts in recovery'. The person with the overactive libido is now a 'sex addict'. Visit a counsellor or therapist and tell them you are suffering from some emotional disorder—say, insecurity and inability to relate to people. The roots of your malady will be traced back to parental influence or supposed traumas of early childhood. You certainly won't be sent away with a breezy, 'You know what's wrong with you? You're too self-obsessed and you stay indoors too much. Go out more, get a hobby and meet more people!'

A pendulum has shifted. Once my vices were sins, and I was a culprit. Now they are diseases and I am an invalid. The problem is, neither of these two extremes feels like the whole truth. The old accusation that people are wilfully immoral fails to recognize that their family, up-bringing, neighbourhood and culture might well predispose them to particular vices. All people are unquestionably sinned against as well as sinning. And the sins of the parents invariably affect the children. This is not hard to demonstrate in contemporary society. Most child abusers were themselves abused in childhood. Many who end up in prostitution were forced into early, inappropriate sexual experiences, or grew up in families where prostitution was the norm. Drug addiction is fuelled by the greed of dealers, and itself spirals into criminality. People are caught up in a web of brokenness beyond their control. Even the young person with an idyllic childhood and loving parents still has to breathe air polluted by heavy industry. We are all, to some extent, victims.

But the current fad for blaming our ills on everything except the person himself is surely equally wide of the mark. We may not be wholly villains, but neither are most of us wholly victims either. In any case, the clear evidence of history shows that to have been a victim is no guarantee of innocence or compassion. Time after time, the first response of victims when they obtain power is to do to others precisely what was done to them. The Hutu of Rwanda, after decades of second-class status, responded by massacring the Tutsi. The Jews, after suffering centuries of victimhood and the horrors of Nazism, in turn treated Palestinians as second-class citizens, denied their historic rights and confiscated land. Many Communists who suffered in Hitler's con-centration camps used exactly the same methods after the war was over—even, in some cases, using the same camps—to eliminate their own enemies.

To present people as if they are only victims has three serious flaws: it undercuts the basis of the entire legal system, it is naïve, and it is demeaning.

Firstly, every system of law has to assume that people are to a large extent morally responsible for their actions. That a man may be a victim of poverty is not an excuse for burglary or assault. That he is a victim of somebody else's bad driving does not excuse his stabbing another motorist. All adults are held to be morally responsible for their actions. Naturally, mitigating circumstances may be taken into account. But no court could possibly conclude that having a rough deal in life makes crime morally acceptable. This is common sense, and the only basis on which a just legal system can operate.

Secondly, the case for innocent victimhood can be naïve, because most people in reality are complex mixtures of recipient and perpetrator. It is dangerous to idealize victims, the poor and the oppressed, as if they are nobler than others. Victims can have just as much capacity for hatred, evil, manipulation and self-pity as the villains who prey on them. Reverse their roles, adjust the circumstances, and watch what happens.

To treat mature adults simply as victims can also be demeaning and patronizing. It is to let people off the hook, to pat them on the back and tell them they cannot help the way they are. As we diminish people's responsibility, we diminish their full humanity. In the long run, this would-be kindness can ultimately be more cruel than the violence and abuse these people have already suffered at the hands of other people and society. It is to collude with their tormentors by telling the victims they cannot now rise above their victimhood and move on. It is to deny them the dignity of being held morally responsible themselves, to deny them a hope of redemption.

Close to our former home in north London, a group of alcoholics sprawls outside the park gates in all weathers. Behind each of the tousle-headed, red-faced individuals lies a sad story of victimhood: difficult home backgrounds, abused childhoods, broken marriages, unemployment, and a sense of personal powerlessness to combat their addiction to alcohol. But to define these people wholly as victims, and so to excuse their behaviour, is to lock them up for ever into a prison of hopelessness. Hope will only come as these victims realize their own complicity in their problems. They need to seize back control of their lives, almost certainly with the help of others, and admit that they may be free to leave their prison. They need to recognize that their physical abuse of their own bodies, and verbal abuse of passers-by, are simply not acceptable and inevitable results of their past. In Christian language, these people—like all of us—are simultaneously sinned against and sinning. True hope will never come through denying the reality of the sin. Rather, it will come through owning up to one's own complicity in the sin, knowing the reality of forgiveness and making a fresh start.

An old Indian proverb says, 'He who cannot dance blames the floor.' It is only as we stop blaming the floor, and work hard at improving our own lack of coordination and failure to practise, that dancing becomes a possibility. To blame the floor—in other words, to see ourselves as victims of circumstances beyond our control—is a cop-out.

Again, we find that the would-be compassion of the secular sceptics turns out to be more cruel and demeaning than the apparently harsh stance they criticize. In any case, it is highly questionable for the sceptics to claim that the biblical doctrine of sin really does treat people just as villains, and not as victims. We shall explore this point further in the next chapter. For now, we need to note simply that the sceptics are wide of the mark. The fact that many people are victims of life does nothing to undermine the Christian doctrine of sin.

Is sin really morbid?

The final sceptical objection we met in Chapter 1 is that people who go on about sin have a problem with pleasure. They are morbid people, who hate to see others enjoying themselves. It is undeniable that sometimes church people have seemed dour and heavy-handed as they railed against sinfulness. This has been for two main reasons: legalism, and a over-pessimistic view of God's creation.

With regard to legalism, we first need to state the obvious: the Christian faith is not lived out in a vacuum. It is always lived out in a concrete, historic setting. From the earliest days of the Church in Roman times, Christians have felt compelled by biblical teaching to take up moral stances that go against the flow of their particular culture. They have particularly dug in their heels on issues of sexuality, life and death (war, infanticide, abortion), wealth and luxury, and entertainments. Christian suspicion of the theatre was particularly strong in periods when it was linked to immorality or pagan idolatry, as in the early centuries of the Christian era. It is true that the way these moral stances have been expressed has sometimes smacked of legalism, as if the Christians who upheld them were against pleasure *per se* (which has rarely been the case, despite popular stereotypes). And it is true that sometimes the Christian faith has attracted legalists. Here, the church has to plead guilty, at least in part.

But the real issue is this: was the Church fundamentally mistaken in its approach of upholding high moral ideals, and censuring those who flouted those ideals? It is hard for some people to answer this question, as their perspective is clouded by a legalistic church upbringing, or by witnessing the worst excesses of such churches. The kind of churches that burned pop records, banned dancing and alcohol, warned of the dire consequences of masturbation and shunned 'worldly' fashions or movies often left a legacy of repression and hurt. But were they, and their forebears in the faith, wrong to insist on moral absolutes at all, or to deal in categories of sin and redemption? Surely not. Their mistake was to be over-zealous in the areas to which they applied these categories, and to apply them to minor, secondary issues. The mistake was not in the categories themselves. Legalism is a personality type, not a biblical way of doing ethics.

The second reason why Christians have seemed morbid and anti-pleasure is that they have sometimes operated with a deficient doctrine of creation. The famous 19th-century American evangelist Dwight L. Moody (1837–99) once said in a sermon, 'I look upon this world as a wrecked vessel. God has given me a lifeboat and said to me, "Moody, save all you can."' As we shall find in the next chapter, Moody was surely right to claim that Christianity is fundamentally a rescue operation.

But this is only one side of how the biblical writers view the world around us. On the one hand, the world is seen as damaged and fallen, in need of rescue; and humanity's defining need is for salvation. On the other hand, it is also God's awe-inspiring creation, which the Maker declared to be good (Genesis 1), and through which the creator may be glimpsed (Psalm 19, Romans 1:20). Humanity is the pinnacle of this wonder-filled creation (Psalm 8). Moody only states one side of this biblical paradox, as have other believers from time to time down the centuries. Here Matthew Fox, whose Creation Spirituality we met in the last chapter, is partly right in his criticism of the Church down the centuries. Christians often have downplayed the wonder and beauty of creation.

When this happens, the result is an excessively negative view of the material world and our embodied human nature as hopelessly damaged, mere fuel for the fires of judgment. As with legalism, here too the church has to plead partly guilty. But again, we need to recognize that this low view of creation and human nature, like the legalistic mindset, is not the outworking of a balanced, biblical Christianity. Each is a distortion produced by people failing to grasp the breadth of the biblical vision, which holds together high moral ideals with a love and compassion for people who fall far short of those ideals, and the fallenness of the material world with an appreciation of its wonder, beauty and revelatory character.

Believing in sin is not morbid—far from it. But those who believe in it may sometimes have been morbid people.

Back to health

So far in this chapter, we have taken a closer look at the sceptics' arguments against the moral foundations which the Christian doctrine of sin has assumed. Each time, we have found their own house to be more rickety, and built on less secure foundations, than the one they are criticizing. Each time, we have seen that the sceptics' alternative views give moral support to tyranny and bigotry, undermining justice and the legal system and, ultimately, denying victims the moral dignity of free people. Far from being morbid, the idea underlying the Church's doctrine of sin—that we are all bound by solid moral obligations—seems the more robust and healthy option. Instead of fudging the issue, sin tells it like it is. It doesn't duck issues of justice and responsibility.

The critics of the idea of sin may superficially sound more compassionate and positive, but they are pointing down a bleak road which leads to lawlessness and loss of hope. Defenders of the idea of sin may superficially sound negative, but they are pointing down a road that opens into wide vistas of hope and dignity.

Is it morbid to talk of cancer? It depends whom you are talking to. If you are sitting in a restaurant with a group of healthy friends, to hold forth on various types of tumours will more than likely dampen the mood of the evening. But what if you are a doctor, sitting opposite a patient whose early signs of cancer you have just diagnosed? Under those circumstances, to refuse to talk of cancer would be heartless, even lethal. For a doctor to help a patient to face up to the reality of her own condition is not morbid. It is the only path that can lead back to health.

Loose ends

There is still one objection that we raised in Chapter 1 which we have not addressed directly. It is the purely factual observation that the idea of sin is not universal. In particular, Eastern faiths (such as Hinduism and Buddhism), native spiritualities (such as that of the native Americans and Australians), and pagan spiritualities (such as Wicca and the Norse tradition) tend to have no emphasis on personal sin in the sense that the Christian tradition does. This is perfectly true. Here, we need to challenge one of our most potent cultural myths head on: the idea that given a range of competing views, either they are all equally 'true' in some way for the person who believes in them, or that none can be true. This is a fad of current thought that is far from self-evident.

For one, the idea that mutually contradictory beliefs can somehow all be 'true', in a way that transcends reason and common sense, is odd in the extreme. Somehow, people today feel they can claim this in the areas of religion and values in a way they don't in other areas. Try telling somebody you are choosing your own biology, or your own laws of physics, and see how they respond. But many people will tell you with confident certainty that the Muslim who believes Jesus was a prophet, the Christian who believes he was God incarnate, and the Buddhist who believes Jesus is irrelevant, are all 'right' in some way, even though the views are flatly contradictory.

The fact that Christians believe in sin whereas Wiccans don't does not prove that both must be 'true' in some personal, mystical sense. It implies rather that one might be mistaken. The idea that because

Christianity and Wicca have different views of sin, both must be equally wrong is similarly odd. It is a conclusion that does not follow from the facts of the matter. The thinking person should weigh up where the evidence seems to point, rather than taking an arbitrary decision in advance that contradicting views mean both are either equally right or equally wrong. That would be to define the whole quest for truth as off-limits, a strange and ultimately pessimistic strategy. Far better, surely, to see which view more closely fits the evidence.

Next, we also need to ask whether belief systems that officially deny sin can live with the implications of their denial, such as the Eastern faiths that stress detachment from the material world. For example, many streams of Hinduism do not believe in a personal god, and hold that sin is an illusion. The only sort of 'error' in the human heart is our ignorance. Yet, at the same time, the Hindu scriptures go into great detail about human sins and outline all sorts of ways of doing penance for them.

Buddhism too denies the existence of God, and rejects the Christian concept of sin. Instead, it claims that what's wrong with the world is our attachment to the illusion that the material world is real. But at the same time, the Buddhist concept of *shila* (control of speech and actions) dictates a very strict moral code which must be followed, to avoid hurting other individuals, society and ourselves. This strict code of ethics, which includes abstaining from killing, stealing, sexual misconduct, false speech and intoxicants, is considered a prerequisite for anybody following the way of the Buddha.

Similarly, the Western Wiccan or neo-pagan claims not to believe in the Christian doctrine of sin, but invariably adheres to a code of moral obligations. Such obligations might include not harming the environment, tolerating other people's lifestyles, and not hurting others. Devotees strive to live by these moral obligations and have a conscience which tells them when they fail, and they expect others to live by them too.

In each case, the belief system rejects the Christian picture of God and human sinfulness, yet its adherents live by a code of moral obligations. This is, of course, what we should expect if the Christian doctrine of sin is true. Even those people whose belief systems officially deny sin are still compelled to live as if it were a reality. For the Christian, this should come as no surprise. In a Christian framework, the God-given moral structure of the universe applies not only to believers, but to all people. The apostle Paul writes that God has created a world that reflects his own moral nature (Romans 1:18–20), and that all people have a God-given conscience that alerts them when they are cutting against his moral order (Romans 2:14–16).

The African white rhino has a little bird, an oxpecker, that perches on its back and feeds on the insects which land on the rhino's tough hide. This oxpecker, a kind of starling, can eat anything up to 2000 insects off a rhino's back each day. The white rhino is notoriously short-tempered and will run at anything that invades its personal space. But it seems happy to put up with the parasitic oxpecker. The reason for this is the rhino's eyesight: white rhinos cannot see over long distances. The oxpecker, on the other hand, has good eyesight and sits high on the rhino's back, so it can see any approaching danger long before it arrives. It provides an early warning system for the rhino by hissing when trouble is on the way.

The Christian view of human nature tells us that we are morally short-sighted, but that we each have an 'oxpecker' perching on our shoulder, hissing in our ear when we are about to do wrong. It is called our conscience.

The clues so far

So far, the clues seem to say this much. Cultures around the world and through history all share a basic, core morality. Likewise, each of us is aware of this same core of moral obligations that are binding on us. We cannot escape a sense of 'ought', expressed through the inner voice of conscience. Even if we deaden our conscience over time, or deliberately do something we know to be wrong, that 'ought' is still inescapable. When we come across somebody who genuinely has no conscience, we recognize a symptom not of a valid alternative morality, but of mental illness. Unless we accept the validity of moral obligations on all people, around the world and through history, we forfeit the right to criticize the evils done by societies, governments, and individuals. And we forfeit the privilege of hearing their criticisms of us. A belief in real moral obligations is vital for our moral health, justice and dignity—as individuals and as a society. The case is strong.

That is why many people today agree that relativism—both cultural and individual—cannot come up with the goods. At the same time, however, they hesitate to accept the Christian belief that universal moral obligations are rooted in the moral character of God. There must be a morality which is solid and universal, they say, and it must be somehow rooted in human nature. Their three main suggestions are that universal morality must be based in either self-interest, evolutionary biology, or human instinct. We must briefly examine each of these proposals more closely.

Self-interest

The first of the three options claims that morality 'pays'. It is in my own self-interest to help others and be kind, because others will then treat me that way, and at the end of the day we are all better off. This sounds superficially plausible, but it does not stand up to scrutiny. We have all experienced moments when our moral 'ought' impels us to do something which is quite clearly contrary to self-interest. If I see a small child fall from an ocean liner into the rough sea, and I am the only adult present, my moral 'ought' tells me to jump in and try to rescue that child, even risking my own life. Of course, I might weigh up the alternatives and decide that my own life is more valuable to me than the child's, and pretend not to have noticed the child fall. But that does not alter the fact that I have made a major effort to silence a moral obligation I am all too aware of. And it means that, in all probability, for years to come my mind will replay that moment and my conscience will remain troubled. I shall very likely spend sleepless nights, judging myself to be the moral equivalent of a murderer.

In fact, my moral obligations more often than not cut against my own self-interest. It becomes rather unreal and nebulous to claim that somehow the greater self-interest of humanity is served by my acting morally, if day by day I experience countless times when I know full well that my own self-interest would be better advanced by overriding my conscience, by doing some discreet cheating, lying, and turning a blind eye to others' needs. This is never truer than with money. My self-interest dictates that I hang on to my cash and try to obtain more. My moral obligations tell me to give more to charity, and to buy costlier fair-trade goods and avoid avarice. Self-interest clearly often conflicts with moral impulses, so it can hardly do as a basis for morals.

Evolution

The second basis proposed is evolutionary biology. In other words, morality has evolved as an aid to survival of the species. But this 'explanation' runs into the same dilemmas as the last one. It is all very well talking in general terms about the well-being and survival of the race, but what I am responsible for is my own day-to-day life. And at that level, my own survival can be clearly jeopardized by my sense of moral obligation to help others, as in the case of helping the drowning child. In addition, evolutionary biology is a strange basis for ethics. If the survival of the species is the bottom line, practices like rape should probably be deemed good and helpful, as should allowing 'weaker specimens', such as disabled people, to die.

But again, our moral 'ought' cuts across what would seem most beneficial for the survival of the race. It certainly offers no explanation of where genuine 'oughts' might have come from, which appear to stand outside natural processes. Evolutionary biologists might have a brave stab at explaining why people *think* they have moral obligations. But they are quite unable to account for how these moral obligations might be real and binding on us.

Instinct

A third attempted explanation for the origins of a sense of morality lies in the area of instinct. But this is the weakest of all three. People feel any number of instincts every day of their lives: hunger, thirst, lust, aggression, anger, tenderness, and countless others. Unless there is a higher standard than instinct, how can we know which instinct to follow and which to refuse? Most people's daily experience of moral impulses is that they cut right against our 'natural' impulses. Again, this attempt at explanation fails to account for our daily experience of morality, an 'ought' that speaks from our conscience, challenging our tendency to give into selfish and inappropriate instincts.

The only alternative

There is only one alternative, an alternative conceded by the atheistic philosopher Jean-Paul Sartre. Sartre stated in his famous book *Existentialism* that 'everything is permissible if God does not exist'. He was admitting that there are only two alternative moral foundations. Either God exists, and is the source of our moral impulses. Or else he doesn't exist, and we are left with an individual relativism, where each person is left to improvise their own morality. Certainly, moral obligations seem very out of place in a world which is merely the result of time and chance. Why these strong impulses, demanding that we override self-interest, evolution and instinct, if time and chance are the only true foundations of life? Our sense of moral obligation certainly *feels* as if it comes from beyond ourselves.

But how does belief in a personal God actually provide us with a secure moral foundation? This point is sometimes misunderstood by moral philosophers and textbooks of ethics, which frequently offer a strange caricature of a Christian foundation for moral obligation, based only on laws and commandments. The way such textbooks tend to express it is like this:

People of faith believe that God has given the world divine commands, which he expects us to keep. But does something become 'right' simply because God is all-powerful, and he commands it? In that case, God becomes a tyrannical despot, enforcing arbitrary commands on the basis of 'might is right'—whether or not they are intrinsically good and moral. Alternatively, does God command something because this action is right in itself? In that scenario, there must be a higher standard than God, to which he has to conform, and that denies God's sovereignty.

Such word-games bear almost no relation to how Christians actually find that God gives a foundation for our moral obligations. In a Christian framework, and according to biblical revelation, God is the origin of all life and personhood. We are made in the image of One whose nature is to be absolutely good and loving. Therefore all people, everywhere, find that to behave in a good and loving way fits in with the deep moral structures of the universe, and our own moral human nature. Our moral obligations are not rooted in some arbitrary commands, but in the nature of a good and personal Creator.

Something remarkable

We are finding something quite remarkable. In the previous chapter, the case against sin seemed overwhelming. The secular sceptics seemed to have the finest house in town. But as we look closer, we find that the foundations on which they are themselves building are considerably weaker. Their two varieties of relativism fail to give a satisfactory account of what we actually experience each day of our lives, that our moral obligations are real. And attempts to explain this away by reference to self-interest, evolution and instinct simply don't come up with the goods. The most satisfying explanation for this moral muddle seems to be that of the theist, the believer in a personal God: that our morality is based in the character of God himself.

In this chapter we have not, of course, *disproved* relativism—in either its cultural or individual varieties. Neither have we disproved the claims of those who believe that moral obligations could have a basis in self-interest, evolution or instinct. Nor have we given a full account of how people should approach the nitty-gritty of ethical decision-making, or evaluated different systems for doing ethics. These questions are beyond the scope of a book like this.

We have attempted something much more modest and preliminary. We have asked whether any sort of moral obligations could ever be binding on us, and whether these same obligations might also apply to anybody other than ourselves. We have asked whether it can even be meaningful to talk of 'right' and 'wrong'. In any previous era of history, such questions would have been met with amusement or disbelief. But in our culture of hyperchoice and relativism, the idea that there might be any truth beyond 'what feels true for me', and any morality beyond 'what seems right to me', comes as a genuine surprise to many people.

We have analysed one of our culture's most popular assumptions: that 'right' and 'wrong' are at best relative terms, that to question any-body else's value-system is judgmental, and that talk of 'sin' is therefore mistaken. We have found that there are all sorts of reasons to believe that our moral impulses are not just relative, that right and wrong have real meaning, and that when we choose to do wrong, our conscience tells us we have broken more than an arbitrary rule of our culture or of our own choosing.

We then asked where this sense of real moral obligations might come from. And we found that naturalistic solutions which see morality as just an instinct or an aid to survival simply don't ring true. Indeed, these obligations which we all share seem to come from a source beyond ourselves, and to correspond to the deep moral structure of the way the world is. That the clues point this way should come as no surprise to the Christian believer—who holds that our human nature, and the way the world is, reflect the moral character of God.

The thinking person looks outwards at the world, and inwards at the state of her own heart. She says, 'I know there are things I should do, and things I shouldn't do. My conscience tells me that good and evil do exist. On a global level, I try to work against oppression, and for justice and compassion. And on a personal level, I try to treat everybody with respect and love. I may not always succeed, but I try my best.'

Her Christian friend replies, 'Of course. You instinctively sense that there's something wrong with our world, and you know you don't always live up to your own moral obligations, as expressed through your conscience. We have a word that accounts for all those feelings. *Sin*.'

CHAPTER 3

Critical of the Christian Critics

I see and approve the better course, but I follow the worse.
OVID, *METAMORPHOSES*

**Whether or no man could be washed in miraculous waters,
there was no doubt at any rate that he wanted washing.
But certain religious leaders in London, not mere materialists,
have begun in our day not to deny the highly disputable water,
but to deny the indisputable dirt.**
G.K. CHESTERTON, *ORTHODOXY*

Sin in the Bible

In Chapter 1 we outlined two sets of arguments against believing in sin.
The first set were the arguments of secular sceptics, who objected to the
moral assumptions underlying the whole idea of sin. In Chapter 2 we
responded to these charges, and found that the sceptics' own foundations may well be less sound than the ones they criticize. The second
set of arguments against sin were those of the Christian critics. We
found believers from a range of church backgrounds claiming that the
old idea of sin may have become an obstacle to communicating the faith
in today's world, and that we should be better off either modifying or
dropping it altogether. In this chapter we shall take a closer look at these
criticisms.

Before we do that, we first need to explore the biblical understanding
of sin. Historic Christianity has always seen the Bible as an authoritative
revelation from God, even if the precise ways we state the nature of that
authority has varied between church traditions and across historical

eras. So an appreciation of how the different biblical writers view sin is vital before we can address specific charges made by Christian critics today.

There is, as we might expect of documents written over thousands of years, a range of emphases from writer to writer. But the level of agreement between the various authors is remarkable, and certain themes recur time after time. The portrait of sin throughout the Bible is made up of five main images: broken relationship, an alien power, a matrix, failure and lawbreaking. We shall explore each of these in turn, before making a few additional observations on the view of sin in scripture. Then we might be in a better position to make an informed response to the Christian criticisms outlined in Chapter 1.

Broken relationship

If one image captures the essence of sin in the Bible, it is that of a personal relationship that has gone profoundly awry.

One of the Bible's most memorable instances of wrongdoing is recorded in 2 Samuel 11, where King David spies on Bathsheba while she bathes. He sleeps with her, gets her pregnant, and then tries to hide the evidence by encouraging Bathsheba's husband Uriah to sleep with her too. When this fails, David arranges for Uriah to be killed, and takes Bathsheba as his own wife. When confronted by Nathan the prophet (2 Samuel 12), David is cut to the heart by his own sinfulness. His prayer to God, recorded in Psalm 51, is a powerful and moving expression of penitence. David confesses his wrongdoing, but in verse 4 of the psalm, he tells God, 'Against you, you only, have I sinned and done what is evil in your sight.'

In what sense has David sinned principally against God? Haven't his victims been Uriah and Bathsheba? The heart of David's sin is directed Godwards for the simple reason that this is where all sin is directed. Sin first and foremost means a broken relationship between us and God. The origins of human sin are traced, in the Bible, to the Garden of Eden. But the sin of Adam and Eve is not first and foremost an act of lawbreaking, the flouting of a divine ban on eating from a forbidden tree. The primal sin is one of ingratitude and mistrust. They choose to doubt

God's promise that he has their best interests at heart, and they choose to go their own way (Genesis 3:1–6). Relationship has been broken before fruit is tasted.

The apostle Paul's most telling term for sin is the Greek word *asebia*, 'ungodliness'. In the early chapters of his letter to the Romans, he addresses the whole question of God's response to human sin. He begins his case by citing not specific instances of lawbreaking, but by outlining the *asebia* (1:18) of people who 'neither glorified him as God nor gave thanks to him' (1:21). In other words, because God's nature is personal, and he is a God of love, sin is turning our back on him and rejecting his love.

To understand the biblical picture of sin, we need to do more than count up the Hebrew and Greek words for sin and draw conclusions from their frequency. We need rather to immerse ourselves in the broad sweep of the biblical narrative. This tells of God's desire to draw all people into a relationship (or 'covenant') with himself, beginning with the people of Israel. The drama and tension of the historical narratives arise from the repeated refusal of relationship. The Old Testament Law is to be the means by which Israel could live as God's covenant people. The prophets call on Israel to return to their covenant relationship. Jesus comes to restore the broken relationship. The New Testament letters explain how Jesus restores the relationship, and Revelation shows the relationship finally restored. The word that encapsulates the refusal of relationship, from the human side, is *sin*.

Something profound and important emerges from the insight that the heart of sin is a broken relationship. It is this: sin is not essentially about doing things that are wrong, or lawbreaking. The word can refer to such actions, but only in the secondary and derivative sense that a broken relationship with God leads to a fragmenting life. We can put this another way, by asking a question: 'What is the opposite of sin?' The biblical answer is not 'being good', or 'keeping the law', but 'relationship'—more specifically, 'loving God', or 'being in God's family'.

Even when Paul is clearly talking about sin as doing things that are wrong, he often speaks in relational terms. He refers to sin as *parakoe*, 'disobedience': 'Through the disobedience of the one man the many were made sinners' (Romans 5:19); and he writes to Corinth on the theme of punishment for 'acts of disobedience' (2 Corinthians 10:6). The relational nature of sin explains the biblical horror of Israel worshipping idols, as this amounts to spiritual adultery. To jump into bed with a host of fertility gods (Judges 2:10–13, and elsewhere) is the ultimate betrayal of covenant relationship, the final infidelity.

The essential biblical framework for getting to grips with sin, then, is a relational one and not primarily a moral one. In that sense, the whole debate of the last chapter—about moral obligations, and knowing right from wrong—was a secondary issue from a biblical perspective. That is not to say it was irrelevant. We shall see below how sin as broken relationship becomes sin as lawbreaking. But lawbreaking is not the heart of the matter. The crucial issue is relationship.

An alien power

Another potent image in the Bible is of sin as a hostile power, an evil enemy or slave-driver who holds us captive or takes us over from within. When God addresses Cain, shortly before he murders his brother Abel, God warns him that he is falling captive to this alien power by giving in to his murderous anger: 'If you do not do what is right, sin is crouching at your door; it desires to have you' (Genesis 4:7).

In John's Gospel, Jesus tells an audience of Jewish converts that 'everyone who sins is a slave to sin' (John 8:34). Paul tells the Christians in Rome that they 'used to be slaves to sin' (Romans 6:15–23), and that sin is an alien power which takes over the body of its victims (rather like the monster in the sci-fi movie, *Alien*!): 'It is no longer I myself who do it, but it is sin living in me' (Romans 7:17). Paul even talks of sin as having an independent will of its own. He pictures sin reigning (Romans 5:21), and 'seizing' an opportunity, and says that this evil, alien presence produced in him 'every kind of covetous desire' (Romans 7:8).

The same image is used by Peter, in his second letter. He describes a particular group of false teachers, saying that 'they mouth empty, boastful words and, by appealing to the lustful desires of sinful human nature, they entice people who are just escaping from those who live in error. They promise them freedom, while they themselves are slaves of depravity—for a man is a slave to whatever has mastered him' (2 Peter 2:18–19).

Paul adds that (again like the monster in the *Alien* movies), unless it is rooted out, this hostile alien power ends up killing its host: 'You are slaves to sin, which leads to death' (Romans 6:16) and, 'The wages of sin is death' (Romans 6:23).

The letter of James speaks in language even more reminiscent of evil alien life-forms taking over a person: 'But each one is tempted when, by his own evil desire, he is dragged away and enticed. Then, after desire has conceived, it gives birth to sin; and sin, when it is full-grown, gives birth to death' (James 1:14–15).

However, adds Paul, it is not just individuals who fall into the grip of the alien power and become its slaves. Rather, 'the whole world is a prisoner of sin' (Galatians 3:22).

Is this alien power the same as the devil? As we shall find in Chapter 5, there is a strong biblical case to be made for the existence of a tempter, a real force of evil in the universe, at work in sinful humanity. But Satan is not centre stage in any of the verses we have just explored. The subject of all these verses is sin itself, personified as a hostile power. It is a way of talking about human sinfulness so as to bring out its alien, predatory and life-consuming character.

A matrix

The biblical picture of sin is not individualistic. Paul writes that when we pull away from our central, defining relationship with God, and we are gripped by an alien power, we are lured irresistibly into a whole network of sick people, places and relationships—a matrix. He tells the Ephesians that in their sinful past they had 'followed the ways of this world' (Ephesians 2:2). Sometimes the New Testament writers use this word 'world' in a neutral way, meaning simply the environment where we all live. But sometimes they use it in a pejorative sense, to mean the entire, interlinked network of a disordered, Christ-rejecting culture.

Paul tells the Corinthians that 'the wisdom of this world is foolishness' (1 Corinthians 3:19). John too warns his readers, 'Do not love the world', tells them that 'the world and its desires pass away', and talks of 'overcoming the world' (1 John 2:15, 17; 5:4–5). Again, James uses not only relational but also matrix language to warn his readers: 'You adulterous people, don't you know that friendship with the world is hatred toward God?' (James 4:4).

Paul is using matrix language when he claims that just as all believers are 'in Christ', so anybody who is a victim of sin is 'in Adam' (*Adam* is Hebrew for 'humankind' in a generic sense). This is his argument in Romans 5:12–19. Belief and unbelief are not simply individual decisions. Rather, believing or not believing each commit us to membership of a whole community: either the life-giving body of Christ, the new humanity, or else the sick and sinful body of Adam, the old humanity.

In the book of Revelation, too, human rebellion against God is a matrix. The focus of rebellion is an evil city, Babylon (ch. 18). Entire governments and religious groups are seen serving the beasts of antichrist (ch. 13). In the Old Testament, sin is similarly shared as well as individual. The prophet Ezekiel can describe the whole city of Sodom as 'arrogant, overfed and unconcerned', adding that 'they did not help the poor and needy' (Ezekiel 16:49). Isaiah confesses that not only is he himself a 'man of unclean lips', he lives among 'a people of unclean lips' (Isaiah 6:5), and he addresses the people of Israel as a nation in shared rebellion: 'Ah, sinful nation, a people loaded with guilt, a brood of evildoers, children given to corruption!' (1:4). When he goes on to explain why he is accusing the whole nation of corporate sin, he also underlines the point that sin centres on broken relationship with God: 'They have forsaken the Lord; they have spurned the Holy One of Israel and turned their backs on him' (1:4).

To quibble over whether absolutely every single individual in these societies really had rejected God is to split hairs. No doubt there were more than a few God-fearing people in each of these places. The prophets' point is simply this: that all groups and societies develop an ethos which is bigger than the sum of their individual parts. A whole corporate body can be infected by sickness, and can be a hothouse where further infection breeds. In our individualistic society, many people find it hard to envisage sin as anything other than individual transgression. Wrong, say the biblical authors. Sin is a whole matrix of warped relationships and shared practices, into which we are drawn and become trapped.

These biblical images of sin as collective are not just wise theological insight. They carry psychological conviction, and they are something we see every day with our own eyes. Sin is not simply an illness which the autonomous individual develops in isolation; people simply don't work that way. Sin is propagated through the web of culture and society, dominated as it is by the 'old humanity'. Governments, nations, companies, families and other groups of people can become progressively corrupted and entangled in webs of deceit. We are all socialized into certain sins by our culture, and these sins can take many forms: alienation, injustice, racism, sexism, nationalism, materialism, promiscuity, violence, greed. It is impossible to draw a boundary line marking where personal sin ends and corporate sin begins. Both are real, and so intertwined as to be inseparable.

The social outworking of sin also causes the big obstacles to our Christian discipleship. Believers can know the glorious reality of sins forgiven, and experience membership of the body of Christ, but the new life has to be lived out in our old, ailing culture. The matrix still draws us to itself and holds us tight. We need to be socialized out of the social habits and shared patterns of sin, just as we were once socialized into them.

However, the antidote to social sin can never lie in changing the social structures alone. Every type of sin begins in the human heart—in the attitude that doubts God's promises and breaks relationship with him—and any viable solution must address the heart-disease of sin. Action to improve society is, of course, always worthwhile. And when accompanied by a call to restored relationship with God, it can be powerful and effective. But social action alone leaves the central dilemma unaddressed: the mystery of the matrix of human sin.

Failure

The Greek word Paul uses most frequently to describe sin is *hamartia*, which means 'missing the mark'. Paul uses this word, for example, in

Romans 5:12, and spells it out clearly in Romans 3:23: 'All have sinned and fall short of the glory of God.' *Hamartia* is borrowed from the language of archery. We try to hit the target, but our arrow goes wide of the mark or falls short. We fail to hit what we were aiming at. In the Old Testament, the most common Hebrew word for sin is *chatha*, which also means 'missing the mark'. Sin is failure to live up to what we could be and were intended to be. We don't reach our full potential.

Historically, many Christians have identified the essence of this failure as *hubris*, pride. Missing the mark can certainly include this sin of puffing oneself up, thinking too highly of oneself, and an urge to dominate others. But equally, it might involve precisely the opposite: failing to have a healthy sense of our own value before God, allowing ourselves to be treated as a doormat by others. Biblically, both extremes are sinful. Both are evidence of missing the mark of what we were created to be.

In Romans 3:23, which we cited earlier ('all have sinned and fall short of the glory of God'), we find Paul underlining another key biblical understanding of sin: that everybody is affected by it. We all fall short, to the extent that 'there is no one righteous, not even one' (Romans 3:10). Paul is echoing Old Testament books such as Proverbs: 'Who can say, "I have kept my heart pure; I am clean and without sin"?' (20:9) and Psalms: 'All have turned aside, they have together become corrupt; there is no one who does good, not even one' (14:3).

John underlines the same point, in his first letter: 'If we claim to be without sin, we deceive ourselves and the truth is not in us' (1 John 1:8). And Jesus himself implies the same thing when he challenges the crowd itching to stone the adulterous woman: 'If any of you is without sin, let him be the first to throw a stone' (John 8:7). All the raised stones fall to the ground.

The biblical account of sin is profoundly democratic, levelling all privilege and human inequality. We are all sinners, who have fallen short of the glory of God. But we hardly need the scriptures to spell this out. That all people, everywhere, fall short of even their own ideals, and that there is no corner of the world where evil is a stranger—these are not simply matters of biblical doctrine. They are a universal experience.

Lawbreaking

Sin, then, is more than anything a broken relationship with God. By extension, we then become prey to an alien power, we get caught up in a warped system, and we miss the mark. But Paul also uses a number of lesser terms for sin, which are more or less interchangeable and all mean breaking the moral law. Sin is *anomia*, 'lawlessness' (Romans 6:19, REB). It is *parabasis*, 'lawbreaking' (Romans 2:23; 5:14), and *paraptoma*, 'trespasses' (Romans 4:25; Ephesians 2:1, NRSV).

In the New Testament, such lawbreaking is not just about specific acts that we do. It is a matter of our whole mindset. The self which is out of relationship with its creator naturally begins to disintegrate, first in its attitudes and then in its actions. Jesus points out that bad fruit grows on a bad tree (Matthew 7:17–20, 12:33), and that adultery and murder happen in the heart long before they erupt into actions: 'You have heard that it was said, "Do not commit adultery." But I tell you that anyone who looks at a woman lustfully has already committed adultery with her in his heart' (Matthew 5:27– 28).

This moral dimension of sin is present, and warned against, in the Bible because God is not only loving: he is also holy, and he calls his people to lives of holiness. The closer we draw to God's brightness, the more our own stains show up. The more we are drawn into God's family of love and acceptance, the more we want to live in a way that will please him. So the pages of this book that were taken up in defending the reality of moral obligations against the attacks of the relativists were not wasted. Sin does include breaking the moral law.

But it is important to underline that sin means lawbreaking only in a secondary and derivative sense. At its heart lies a broken relationship which then, by extension, leads to the disintegration of the self and a disordered lifestyle. This disorder is then clear for ourselves and everybody else to see, as we break the moral law.

To put things another way: the big problem is *sin*, which then leads to *sins*. This emphasis distinguishes biblical Christianity from law-based faiths such as Islam. Islam shares the Christian belief in sins (as acts of lawbreaking), but rejects the biblical perspective that we inherit a universal bias toward sin. In the Muslim worldview, people are born innocent. The root of lawbreaking is not sin, but human weakness. People simply make wrong choices. The antidote to sin is not salvation but better guidance in keeping God's commandments, as revealed in the Qur'an, and in making penance for lapses.

Christians respond that any religion based on obedience to law misses the point. We respect the faith of our Muslim friends, share with them a common enemy in secularism, and hold similar views on many aspects of ethics. But one of the crucial points on which we differ profoundly is over our different understandings of human nature. The issue is not that people need to be more observant in keeping divine commands, says biblical Christianity. It is that human nature itself is fundamentally corrupted. We cannot keep God's law, however hard we try and however religiously educated we might be. Nothing less than a transformation of human nature from within will be radical enough to address the scale of the problem. Sins are merely a symptom of something bigger: sin.

Scum of the earth

We have found that in the Old Testament, and in the New Testament letters, there is a pattern to how the word 'sin' is used. Sin centres on a broken relationship with God, which leads to our being held in the grip of an alien power, participating in a matrix of evil, failing to hit the mark; and, as our lives disintegrate, we break the moral law. And we have found that sin affects all people, everywhere. But when we come to the Gospels, we seem to find something rather surprising.

In the Gospels, the word often appears to designate not a universal human condition of alienation, but a particular category of immoral person. Jesus visits the house of a Pharisee called Simon and, while he is there, a prostitute pours oil over his feet. Simon mutters, 'If this man were a prophet, he would know who is touching him and what kind of woman she is—that she is a sinner' (Luke 7:39). 'Sinner' is a term applied in the Gospels to prostitutes and tax collectors (see Luke 18:13; 19:7), to Gentiles (Mark 14:41; Luke 6:32–34) and even to

Jesus, when the Pharisees accuse him of breaking Sabbath regulations (John 9:16, 31).

What we are seeing here is a very specific use of the term, to refer to individuals or groups of people in first-century Jewish society who did not keep the commands of the Jewish Torah, or Law. It reflects a particular usage of the Jewish religious authorities, rather than the general portrait of sin through scripture. Some modern translations helpfully print these specific uses of the term 'sinner' in the Gospels in inverted commas, to draw attention to this very specific, contextualized sense. The New Living Translation even gets the message across by using the word 'scum': 'The Pharisees were indignant. "Why does your teacher eat with such scum?" they asked his disciples' (Matthew 9:11).

Coming to faith

There is one more issue worth noting, which is how sin relates to evangelism. Through the pages of the Bible, we are left in no doubt that what is wrong with the human heart, and the whole world, is sin, and that the death of Jesus Christ was in some sense a death for the sin of the world (an idea we shall return to in Chapter 5). But can individuals necessarily only come to a saving faith in Christ after they have faced up to the full horrors of their sinful state?

In other words, salvation may be the answer to sin, but does somebody have to have been asking the sin question before they can understand the salvation answer? Clearly, this has major issues for how we share the faith today. If it turns out that, biblically, people *always* have to have their noses rubbed in an awareness of their sin before they can come to faith, that would set a strong precedent for us to follow. Certainly, the classic evangelical 'testimony' of the journey to faith has a familiar movement: from a sordid life of sin to sweet salvation. The testimonies of many well-known Christian leaders down the centuries have followed just this pattern: John Newton, the 18th-century slave-trader; Billy Bray, the 19th-century Cornish alcoholic; Nicky Cruz, the 20th-century street-fighter.

However, if we look at New Testament examples of people coming to faith in Christ, no clear pattern emerges. Some individuals seem to be confronted by a sense of sin first, but not all. In fact, those who do come to faith this way seem to be the exception rather than the rule. So where does the classic evangelical model of being cut to the heart by a sense of sin, and then turning to Christ for a remedy, come from? One thing is clear: the New Testament language of coming to faith does assume that what we are converted out of is sin.

Paul's *magnum opus* on the human condition and God's grace is his letter to the Romans. The whole structure of the book begins by stating the bad news of sin in all its horror, before explaining how Christ can be the answer to sin. The first recorded statement of Jesus in Mark's Gospel, which set the tone for his whole ministry, includes the words, 'Repent and believe the good news!' (Mark 1:15). Repentance, turning away from sin and to the wonder of new life in relationship with God, remains a central theme for Jesus: 'There is rejoicing in the presence of the angels of God over one sinner who repents' (Luke 15:10) and, 'Unless you repent, you too will all perish' (Luke 13:3).

In some conversions, we see such repentance happening before our eyes. The conversion of Zacchaeus the tax collector involves turning from a life in the grip of sin, and turning to Christ (Luke 19:1–10). The symbolic parable of the prodigal son (Luke 15:11–32) exhibits all the main characteristics of sin we have already explored. The son has a broken relationship with his father, he is in the grip of overwhelming and destructive craving, he gets caught in a web of sinful relationships, he falls short of his birthright, and breaks the moral law (not least because demanding his inheritance means effectively wishing his father dead).

When Paul and Barnabas speak in Lystra, they tell the people to turn from their worthless false gods to the one true God (Acts 14:15), just as Paul reminds the Thessalonians how they were converted 'from idols' (1 Thessalonians 1:9). In both instances, Paul's description of conversion entails turning from the 'power' of another god and its warped matrix, and a turning to restored relationship with God. He describes conversion, in other words, as a turning from sin. However, despite the fact that the classic repentance formula ('repent and believe') is used often, we find surprisingly few actual Zacchaeuses and prodigal sons in the New Testament.

If we look at Peter and the other disciples, it is hard to point to any clear pattern of turning from sin and turning to Christ. Their 'conversions' seem more gradual, and to be sparked more by the attractiveness of Jesus than to any felt need for forgiveness. When Jesus first calls them, the only thing they leave behind is their fishing-nets!

Peter in particular seems to grow in commitment by a series of leaps and crises: his instinctive dropping of his fishing-net to follow Jesus (Mark 1:16–18), his statement that Jesus was the Messiah (Mark 8:27–30), his trauma at realizing he has denied Jesus (John 18:15–27), running to the empty tomb (John 20:3–8), meeting the risen Jesus at the lakeside (John 21), the Day of Pentecost (Acts 2), the bewildering encounter with Cornelius that makes him reassess his whole theology (Acts 10), and so on. If we try to pin down Peter's single 'moment of conversion', or 'repentance', we find that such categories don't really fit.

Early in Luke's Gospel we read that Peter (then still called Simon) kneels before Jesus and says, 'Go away from me, Lord; I am a sinful man!' (Luke 5:8). But this awareness of his own sinfulness is sparked by the miracle of the full nets of fish (5:1–7). Peter here reflects a common biblical pattern. People are first filled with awe and wonder at encountering the glory that is Christ, which then makes them all too aware of their own inadequacies and need for salvation.

The conversion of the Philippian jailer (Acts 16:25–34) seems to be caused not by an awareness of sin, but because he is shaken to his boots by the earthquake and the miracle he has just seen. The royal official of John 4:43–54 is converted by experiencing Jesus's healing power, as is the man born blind (John 9). Paul's converts in Athens show no awareness of sin. Their response is to Paul's incisive presentation of the gospel, drawing on the Athenians' own poets and philosophers (Acts 17:16–34). Paul's pitch in Athens is not to persuade the cultured Athenians that they are sinners in need of a saviour. Instead, he identifies key enigmas from their own culture and literature, and offers Christ as a clue that makes sense of it all.

Even Paul, whose letters provide our archetypal model of sin and repentance, seems not to have been overwhelmed by sin before his own conversion. He already believed in God, expected the Messiah, was scrupulous in keeping his moral obligations (Philippians 3:4–6). There is no real evidence that he was guilt-ridden or disillusioned with his Judaic heritage. Any sense of his own sinfulness appears to have come *after* his Damascus Road experience. Like so many others in scripture, Paul's conversion is essentially a turning to the wonder of who Christ *is*. For those who come to faith, a sense of what Christ has *done* (in overcoming sin) is doubtless there too, but this tends to be subsequent and secondary.

Some defenders of the more traditional approach will point out that Jesus frequently warns of hell for those who remain stubbornly un-repentant, such as in Matthew 10:28—'Rather, be afraid of the One who can destroy both soul and body in hell'—and in his hard-hitting parable of the sheep and goats (Matthew 25:31–46). Such references, they claim, show that his method of evangelism was, in fact, to warn people of the bad news of sin and its consequences—before going on to give the good news of salvation. However, a closer look at the relevant passages in the Gospels (such as those just mentioned, and Luke 12:4–5; 16:19–31) shows them to be addressed not to unbelievers, but to his own disciples. At most, we can say that Jesus' warnings about continuing in sin are given to motivate believers to evangelize, not to scare unbelievers in.

The other flaw in the argument that Jesus' main evangelistic method was to underline people's sinfulness is that it simply doesn't fit the Jesus of the Gospels. There, we find primarily an invitation to life in all its fullness, a gateway into the Kingdom of God, not so much an escape route from hell: 'Come to me, all you who are weary and burdened, and I will give you rest' (Matthew 11:28). Many biblical characters, such as the Samaritan woman in John 4, are visibly drawn to Jesus for precisely this reason.

A major church report from 1992, *Finding Faith Today* (Bible Society), revealed that 49 per cent of UK Christians came to Christ with no previous sense of sin at all, and only 18 per cent felt guilty about a particular thing they had done wrong. This should not surprise us. It reflects the normal biblical picture of conversion, which is first and foremost rooted in wonder, gratitude or love for Jesus Christ. The full implications of what he has done seem to sink in over time. As we noted at the start of Chapter 1, even the Puritan Jonathan Edwards, for all his classic Calvinist theology, normally appealed to the glory and wonder of Christ, rather than to the horribleness of sin. His 'Sinners in the Hands of an Angry God' sermon was the exception rather than the rule.

The challenges of the Christian critics

We might now be in a better position to explore the criticisms levelled by Christians against traditional approaches to sin, as outlined in the first chapter. These critics represented a range of different Christian traditions, but they were united in their belief that the whole idea of sin is an obstacle. Specifically, they attacked it as unbiblical, putting the theological emphasis in the wrong place, giving a wrong picture of God, hindering outreach and being over-individualistic. Will their critique turn out to be as wrong-headed and unlivable as the scepticism of the secularists, or can we give a thumbs-up for some of the points at which they want to challenge received tradition and revise unhelpful popular stereotypes?

Is sin really unbiblical?

Firstly, can we really say, after all we have said about sin in the Bible, that sin is an unbiblical idea? It is possible to make a case that all the above references together constitute only a minor theme in scripture, to be found mainly in the writings of Paul. And it is possible to claim that if we focus on the original Jesus, we shall find that he principally brought a superior moral code (the view of Pelagius and Harnack), came to show people how to improve their attitude and tap their full potential (the view of Peale and Schuller), or that Jesus was a 'Cosmic Christ', who taught us—far from dwelling on 'original sin'—to celebrate God's 'original blessing' and the interconnectedness of creation (as suggested by Fox).

In theory, any of these three challenges to traditional theology could be true. The biblical writers sometimes do leave us to wrestle with apparent contradictions, rather than giving us a neat, easy compromise position. If any of these critics are right, maybe we just have to live with a paradox that the Bible says a lot about sin, but the real heart of the human dilemma lies elsewhere. However, if we study the ways Jesus is portrayed in the New Testament, this idea that sin is a marginal issue hardly stands up.

Zechariah, father of John the Baptist, prophesies that his son will prepare the way for God's chosen one by giving the people 'the knowledge of salvation through the forgiveness of sins' (Luke 1:77). Before the birth of Jesus, the angel tells Joseph to call his new son Jesus, 'because he will save his people from their sins' (Matthew 1:21). Jesus cries out to the people of Galilee, 'Repent and believe' (Mark 1:15). He reveals his priorities by telling the paralysed man, 'Son, your sins are forgiven' (Mark 2:5). He says that the Holy Spirit will be sent to 'convict the world of guilt in regard to sin and righteousness and judgment' (John 16:8). Clearest of all, during his last supper with his disciples, Jesus explicitly states that the wine and bread in his hands are images of a sacrificial death—a broken body and shed blood. He makes it plain that his own imminent death is 'for the forgiveness of sins' (Matthew 26:26–29).

Similarly, from the very earliest days of the Church, the heart of the message proclaimed was one of sin and forgiveness. On the day of Pentecost, immediately after the Spirit has fallen on the small band of believers, Peter tells the crowds, 'Repent and be baptized, every one of you, in the name of Jesus Christ for the forgiveness of your sins' (Acts 2:38). When the high priest in Jerusalem summons the apostles to account for their behaviour, since he had ordered them not to preach about Jesus, they tell him that they are compelled to preach, as Jesus died and was raised 'that he might give repentance and forgiveness of sins' (Acts 5:31). When Paul describes his Damascus Road experience to King Agrippa, he quotes the words of Jesus himself: Paul is to be sent out to unbelievers 'that they may receive forgiveness of sins' (Acts 26:18).

Another pointer in the same direction is the imagery of blood sacrifice that surrounds Jesus, picking up on Old Testament images of atonement. John the Baptist describes Jesus as 'the Lamb of God, who takes away the sin of the world' (John 1:29). The whole of the letter to the Hebrews is an extended meditation on how Jesus fulfils the Jewish sacrificial system, by making a full and final atonement for the sins of the people (Hebrews 2:17). Peter explains that Jesus 'bore our sins in his body on the tree' (1 Peter 2:24). John, author of Revelation, says that Jesus is the one who 'has freed us from our sins by his blood' (Revelation 1:5), and sees Christ in the paradoxical form of a sacrificial lamb who is also king and judge (chs. 5—6).

Wherever we look in the New Testament, we find Jesus offered as the antidote to human sin. And we find Jesus presented as the definitive answer to the sin problem as it finds expression in the Old Testament. Jesus is the new Adam, who regains what was lost in Eden through sin (Romans 5); he is the ultimate sacrifice for sin, the climax of the sacrificial system (Hebrews); what the Law of Moses could not achieve because of human sin, Jesus made a reality (Romans 8:1–4; Galatians 5). A Jesus who is not profoundly linked to the problem of human sin is not the Jesus of the Bible.

Back in 1937, the US theologian H. Richard Niebuhr summarized the liberal theology of his day in scathing terms: 'A God without wrath brought men without sin into a kingdom without judgment through the ministrations of a Christ without a cross.' Niebuhr's words summarize well the results of all attempts to invent a new Christianity which is not based around the problem of sin and humanity's need for salvation. The result is something no longer recognizably Christian.

We can put this another way, by asking a provocative question: 'What is the difference between spirituality and entertainment or recreation?' To ask such a question will strike some people as odd, even offensive. But reflect on this for a moment. If we claim that spirituality is essentially about inducing moods of tranquillity, so is much classical music. If we say it is about feeling united with creation, so is gardening. If we say it is about a sense of wonder, or contact with intelligence beyond our own, so is science fiction. If we say it is about ecstasy, being drawn beyond ourselves, so is sex. If it is the thrill of contemplating encounter with non-human intelligence, so is UFOlogy. And if we say it is an encounter with the exotic and thrilling, so is a trip to Marrakesh. What is distinctive about spirituality? What does it offer that no form of entertainment or recreation ever could? The historic Christian answer to that question is 'forgiveness of sin'. Any form of 'spirituality that does not have at its heart experiencing or living out forgiveness of sin lacks something essential. It risks becoming a form of spiritual entertainment, a search for warm, fuzzy feelings.

Unfortunately, some Christians have interpreted the clear emphasis on sin in the Bible to mean that human beings are as bad as they could possibly be, and that we are rotten through and through. This has been the tone of some preaching down the years, but this is equally wide of the mark. The other side of the same coin, for the biblical writers, is that people are the pinnacle of God's creation, made in the image of God himself (Genesis 1:26–27), fearfully and wonderfully made (Psalm 139:14), little lower than heavenly beings, crowned with glory and honour, rulers over the earth (Psalm 8:4–6). God cares intimately for all his creatures, especially human beings (Matthew 6:26–30).

People are a walking paradox: possessors of dignity, value and potential, but also fatally flawed and in need of grace. Sin means that some degree of brokenness or alienation is there in all our relationships: with God, other people, the earth and even ourselves. Even at our best, we are never wholly free from mixed motives. The theologian Reinhold Niebuhr (older brother of Richard Niebuhr, cited earlier), accurately speaks of 'the majesty and the tragedy of human life'.

To be a Christian is to hold on to both poles of the paradox at the same time. To resolve this paradox by saying that we are either all good, and full of our own unlimited potential (in our lifestyle, spirituality or whatever), or else all bad, without dignity or value, is to fall off the map on either side. The Pelagian rejection of the 'miserable worm' tradition of the faith is understandable, but it pushes the pendulum too far the other way, out beyond biblical boundaries. In the New Testament Paul and John hold on to both ends of the paradox well: 'But God demonstrates his own *love* for us in this: While we were still *sinners*, Christ died for us' (Romans 5:8); 'He *loved* us and sent his son as an atoning sacrifice for our *sins*' (1 John 4:10).

It would not be accurate to conclude from the biblical insight that sin is also a matrix that, therefore, all human systems and groups are as bad as they could possibly be. This is clearly not the case. It is simply to affirm that no network of people is immune from sin, any more than individuals can be. Some groups will show horrific evidence of sin in undiluted form: the Khmer Rouge, racial supremacist groups, corporations that exploit impoverished workers, abusive families, gangs of school bullies. Other groups are tainted with subtler forms of sin: political parties that make promises they cannot keep, plumbers who fail to declare income to the taxman, church members who gossip in the name of sharing 'Christian concern'. No group is immune from sin, for the simple reason that all groups are made up of sinful people. And sometimes a group can act as a breeding ground for bigger sins, a corporate evil that goes beyond the sum of its individual members.

The biblical understanding of human nature could be presented as something like a great mansion which has fallen into a state of ruin and become damaged, overgrown and dangerous. Pelagian optimism is blind to the decay and collapsing masonry, and denies that any drastic renovation is needed. On the other hand, some Christian preachers have come across as being blind to the sheer magnificence of the ruin, and have failed to appreciate the depth of love that the owner still has for it. It is not that the owner, God, simply has the legal title deeds over the mansion, viewing it clinically as a piece of real estate. Rather, he loves it with a passion and feels deep compassion for its ruined state. He loves that old mansion so much that he cannot bear to see it left as a ruin, and is carrying out a painstaking work of restoration.

Has the emphasis really been in the wrong place?

The second criticism of sin comes from some Pentecostal and charismatic Christians, who claim that the traditional emphasis on sin and salvation is right, but not where the real action is. The event that shapes and impacts the Church today, they say, is the outpouring of the Spirit at Pentecost. The cross of Jesus is a necessary station on the way to it, but not a terminus. We need to enter into a new realm of the power of the risen Christ. The major emphasis in preaching, worship times and home groups therefore shifts to the gifts of the Spirit, such as healing, tongues and words of knowledge, encountering the Spirit in power, and so on.

It should be clear from our outline of the biblical picture of sin that such a scenario, for all its current popularity, is inadequate. It is not so much that it is wrong (Pentecost is real; the Spirit does meet people in power, and distributes his gifts lavishly), but that it places an over-emphasis on one part of the Christian life, at the expense of the heart of it. The great Reformer Martin Luther used to contrast a 'theology of the cross', centred on the crucified Jesus, with a 'theology of glory' which tried to bypass or marginalize the cross. Author Tom Smail says of Luther:

(He) knew very well that our sinful hearts are forever devising ways of evading the cross, because it is there that we are most radically judged in order that we may be most radically forgiven... In our present context, therefore, we need to be on guard in case, without any conscious intention, we should begin to evade the cross by devising and promoting a charismatic theology of glory. A spirit who diverts us from the cross into a triumphant world in which the cross does not hold sway may turn out to be a very unholy spirit.
CHARISMATIC RENEWAL (SPCK 1995), P. 58

Smail instead points to what he calls a *paschal* model of Christian renewal, which remains firmly cross-centred. Smail emphasizes the closeness between Jesus and the Spirit, that the risen Jesus still bears the marks of crucifixion, that the Spirit is given for the forgiveness of sins (John 20:22–23), and that the Spirit will never lead us beyond the cross of Christ but always brings us back to it.

He also critiques the emphasis in some church circles on the idea of God dealing with evil by unleashing superior fire power on it, in 'power encounters'. Rather, says Smail, Jesus dealt with evil by absorbing its destructive force in his own body on the cross. True power—to dethrone sin, to restore, renew and heal—always centres on the death and resurrection of Jesus, and on sacrificial love (1 Corinthians 13). One implication of this, Smail suggests, is that those in charismatic leadership should be less ready to call down 'more power!' on themselves and their congregations, and more ready to ask for more of the sacrificial love of God embodied at Calvary. That is where true power lies.

Does it really give a wrong picture of God?

Some Christian critics believe that a focus on sin gives a wrong picture of God, as a wrathful lawgiver and judge. This, they say, is contrary to the central biblical revelation that God is a loving Father. If the biblical definition of sin were simply lawbreaking, this complaint would be right on target. As it is, we have found that the primary definition of sin is broken relationship—precisely the argument these critics are underlining. As such, this family focus is a helpful corrective to those traditions in the Church which have majored on lawkeeping and law-breaking, and have emphasized legal metaphors to explain the significance of the death of Christ. The defining metaphors in scripture are relational. Sin is essentially about a rejection of love.

From this more balanced perspective, even the references to the wrath of God at human sinfulness (such as Romans 1:18; John 3:36) take on a new aspect. Rather than God's wrath being the cold verdict of an impartial judge, it becomes the passionate anger of a loving Father at anything that breaks up his family, anything that seduces away and damages his children. Even God's anger is motivated by love. Salvation, too, is not some legal transaction, but the homecoming of a prodigal son. We shall say more about this theme of God's wrath in Chapter 6.

These critics, then, are on target in their criticisms. But what is undermined by their criticisms is not so much the biblical account of sin, but rather the tendency in some church circles to narrow the definition of sin to lawbreaking.

Does it really hinder outreach?

Christian critics who claim that an undue focus on sin is offputting to unbelievers usually have one very specific model of evangelism in mind, against which they are reacting. It is that of the street evangelist, who waves his black Bible at passers-by, shouting about sin in the hope that his hearers will be so overwhelmed by the bad news about their condition that they will enquire what they must do to be saved. This is another model in which sin tends to be narrowed down simply to lawbreaking. We have noted that this whole approach to street evangelism is based, not unreasonably, on the 'repent and believe' formula commonly found in the New Testament.

However, we also found that few people in the New Testament actually seem to have come to faith in Jesus Christ that way. It appears to be far more common for people to be overwhelmed by a sense of wonder in the presence of Christ, to be healed by him, or to find in him the answer to the unresolved dilemmas of their own culture. Repentance of personal sins unquestionably has its place in the life of faith. But it appears to be the exception to see an acute sense of one's own sin and need for forgiveness as the entry point to faith, either in the New Testament or today.

We can picture historic Christianity as a building that contains a whole host of vital truths about who God is, and about who we are. One of these vital truths is the fact that we are sinners, in need of a saviour. Everybody who enters the bulding discovers that in coming to Christ, they have a sin problem that has been dealt with on the cross. However, this building has many entry doors, each with a different notice above it. One entrance bears a notice which reads, 'Jesus brings inner peace'. Another reads, 'Jesus brings healing'. Another reads, 'Jesus provokes a sense of wonder'. Another reads, 'Jesus is the heart of spirituality'. Another reads, 'Jesus helps me live with integrity'. And yet another, 'Jesus forgives my sins'. You find still more entry doors as you continue walking around the building. Different people enter the building of faith via different doors. That is quite acceptable. It is the New Testament model.

This group of critics, then, is right to criticize one particular approach to outreach. A pattern of evangelism led by personal sin and guilt alone will not generally be helpful. At best, it will only appeal to that minority of unbelievers who are already wrestling with a sense of their own wrongdoing. Our outreach can appeal with a clear conscience to a vast range of felt needs, and can be targeted in specific ways to specific groups of people. We might, for example, lead on a quite different theme if we were talking to a group of prisoners, recent divorcees, students, city businesswomen, or Hindu holy men.

Nevertheless, we shall find that a broader-based, biblical understanding of sin will actually help our evangelism to the varied groups in today's culture. To explain that sin is about broken relationships will connect with the many who are lonely and alienated. To talk of sin as a power which grips and paralyses us might make perfect sense to an addict. To show how we are each caught up in a matrix of wrongdoing makes good sense in a society that finds it easier to identify social evils than personal sins. And in a society where many feel insecure and inadequate, to talk of sin as failure and missing the mark, and an active conspiring in our own downtrodden state, is likely to ring all sorts of bells. Ironically, then, a biblical understanding of sin may well be just the resource we need for culturally sensitive outreach.

Christians who believe that all talk of sin is a hindrance to outreach make a basic error of categories. They slide from saying (reasonably enough) that our evangelistic strategy need not major on sin, to denying that sin is our problem at all. Our biblical survey did not leave this option open to us. The heart of the human problem is sin, in all its varied forms. Enter the building of faith, and there you will find a robust understanding of sin and salvation. But to get there, a person might have gone through any one of a number of doors.

Is sin really individualistic?

By now, it will be clear that the Christian critic who claims that the idea of sin is individualistic is again assuming a definition of sin limited to personal wrongdoing. And as a criticism of this position, it may be quite accurate. In Christian history, sin sometimes has been viewed solely as my own personal wrestling with evil, as purely an individual temptation to lawbreaking. We noted in Chapter 1 how many of the classic statements of sin, such as the so-called Seven Deadly Sins, assume this model, and it has been the assumption behind much popular preaching down the ages.

By now it will also be clear that this is inadequate as a balanced description of the biblical pictures of sin. These include the idea that sin is a whole matrix or environment in which we are embedded. Sin can be corporate as well as individual, affecting families, neighbourhoods, companies and nations. Once again, the critics offer a helpful corrective to an unbalanced, uncritical picture of sin as a single person doing something wrong. As we have found, the biblical doctrine proves to be broader, more incisive and more up to date than its critics (and even many of its would-be defenders) care to admit.

The mystery of origins

In Chapter 6 we shall return to the five images of sin outlined in this chapter to find out about how, in the Christian understanding, God has acted decisively to do something about sin. But before we look at the solution, we need to address a couple more questions about sin: about its origins, and how it is passed on. In the next chapter, we explore the important question: if it is true that the heart of the human problem is sin, then where did it come from? And can any thinking person today seriously believe ancient stories about forbidden trees and talking snakes?

CHAPTER 4

Adam, Eve and Origins

If there be a God, *since* there is a God, the human race is implicated in some terrible aboriginal calamity. It is out of joint with the purposes of its creator. This is a fact, as true as the fact of its existence; and thus the doctrine of what is theologically called original sin becomes to me almost as certain as that the world exists, and as the existence of God.

CARDINAL JOHN HENRY NEWMAN

Bye-bye, Adam

Back in 1997, my book *God, Sex & Generation X* (Triangle) was reviewed in the *Church Times* newspaper. The reviewer, another Anglican clergyman, wrote that he enjoyed the style of the book, and found my comments on contemporary culture pertinent. What he simply couldn't stomach were the assumptions behind its theology, which he airily dismissed as a 'spiced-up fall–redemption package'. He went on to add, 'Surely we have arrived at where we are culturally because we have entered a complicated phase in human evolution, not because we have fallen.'

That reviewer is not alone in sounding as if he is brushing aside the whole notion of a historic fall from innocence into sin. The controversial former Anglican Bishop of Newark, Jack Spong, states bluntly in his book *Rescuing the Bible from Fundamentalism* (HarperCollins, 1991) that the traditional account of a fall in the Garden of Eden 'no longer makes sense', any more than the traditional picture of Jesus Christ dying for sin makes sense today. Such views, he says, are 'ludicrous' and 'repugnant' (p. 234). Spong suggests that evolutionary theory reveals the idea of the fall to be a primitive myth which is untenable for thinking people. He asks, 'Are not the human qualities we now call selfishness or self-centredness the result of the drive to survive far more than of the fall into sin?' He proposes that far from seeing sinful impulses as an alien intrusion into a pristine creation, 'is it not more accurate to say that they were part of creation itself...?' (p. 34).

Spong's approach is common these days. Adam has been given the cold shoulder, by many scientists and theologians alike. In terms of science, the earth is generally understood to be millions of years old, and human beings to have been around for hundreds of thousands of years, having evolved from earlier, pre-human ancestors. And in much contemporary theology, the opening chapters of Genesis tend to be read in *existential* terms. In other words, the accounts of Adam and Eve in Eden are written in the language of ancient myth or saga, with a personal meaning that does not rely on any kind of historical root for its power. No real event is being retold (in either literal or symbolic language). Nor are we dealing with a cosmic event which affected the whole of nature. Rather, the early part of Genesis becomes an archetypal story, a paradigm of our own sinfulness. It tells a story in which I see reflected my own turning away from God, my own vulnerability to temptation, my own capacity for deceit, and so on. The early parts of Genesis are a mirror in which I see my own face.

The baby and the bath water

At first glance, this reworking of the story of the fall seems enormously appealing to the modern mindset. Many people are happy to leave Eden in the realms of ancient myth, and from the story to extract a personal, existential message for themselves. But few go further in exploring the full implications of what they have done. And the implications of taking this course really are immense, especially for Christian theology and ethics.

Whatever else it did, the traditional account of the fall of Adam and Eve proclaimed loud and clear a crucial claim about the way human nature is, and the way the world is: people are not how they are supposed to be. The world is not the way it is meant to be. Things were created good, and subsequently went bad. On this foundation, traditional Christian theology was then able to give a coherent account of human sinfulness. And, importantly, it gave an account of it while preserving the biblical insistence that God is pure goodness, and that he owns no dark or 'shadow' side (1 John 1:5).

This whole issue can be expressed in a question: if God really is good and holy, how can there be such a thing as evil in his world? One possible answer is to say that there is no God at all, of any description. Another option is that there is a god, but he is not wholly good—maybe he mixes good and evil, rather like the pantheons of gods in the ancient world and some Eastern religions. Both these options are possible, but they come fraught with problems, such as the one we touched on in Chapter 2. If the bottom line in the universe is amoral, and our only real motivation is survival or self-interest, then where do we get our inescapable sense of moral obligations from? The other option is to insist that God is good, but that his creation is out of line with his purposes. This is the option historic Christianity has always underlined through a belief in a fall.

Once you remove any idea of a space–time fall, you undercut the whole traditional Christian argument that evil and suffering are alien intrusions in a previously good creation. Not only that, you have to conclude that evil and suffering are created and willed by God, and are either good or necessary parts of the cosmos. On this understanding, whatever happens is simply part of the unfolding evolutionary providence of God. Natural disasters, the bloodiness of the animal world, evils such as rape, racism, child abuse and road accidents then refuse to be traced back to fallen human nature and wrong choices. If God really is all-powerful, these must be every bit as much an intended part of his creation as flowers, love and music. God must have set up a world where these are the normal state of affairs. To work against the effects of sin and suffering may well be to work against the designs of God himself.

To reject the traditional Christian insistence that people were created good and fell is to conclude that God is not wholly good at all (or that he is good, but weak and inept, which is essentially to deny that he is

God). Some radical Christian theologians have made precisely this inference. Paul Ricoeur resignedly concludes, 'We must therefore have the courage to incorporate evil into the epic of hope. In a way that we know not, evil itself cooperates, works toward, the advancement of the Kingdom of God' ('Guilt, Ethics and Religion', in *The Conflict of Interpretations*, Northwestern University Press, 1970, p. 439). John Hick claims that God created people in a 'fallen' state (*Evil and the God of Love*, Macmillan, 1985, p. 280), and Martin Israel that evil is 'an integral part of creation', whose creator is 'necessarily the effector of evil also' (*Angels*, SPCK, 1995, pp. 79, 85). Theologians influenced by Jungian psychology in particular talk of the need to accept the 'darker' side of our world and our human nature, as part of the totality of creation. Faced with the dilemma of what this implies about God, they resort to slippery phrases about the 'dark side of God', or about embracing the 'paradox of God's nature'. If the revisionists are right, it becomes impossible to hold on to the biblical picture of God's utter holiness.

The Freudian claim that what we call 'sin' in human beings is a hangover from an earlier, animal phase of evolution (an argument also used by Cambridge scientist-turned-theologian F.R. Tennant in the first half of the 20th century) also fails to do justice to human experience. We are simultaneously far nobler and far more evil than that implies. Read a personal account of everyday life in Pol Pot's Cambodia or Hitler's Germany, both of which I did recently. Then try to equate the conscious and systematic brutality of those regimes with the instinct within a lion to catch and eat its prey. Such analogies do a serious disservice to the animal kingdom. Even the back-biting, gossip and intrigue of the office or classroom are of a wholly different order from anything found among animals.

But humans combine this capacity for the most appalling and knowing evil with a capacity for acts of astonishing kindness and selfless heroism—such as the English nursery schoolteacher Lisa Potts rushing to protect the schoolchildren in her care from a machete-wielding maniac who broke into the school grounds. Again, these are of an entirely different order from a simple animal instinct to survive or nurture one's young. To collapse sin into an evolutionary animal regression simply doesn't ring true, any more than it rings true to collapse morality into mere survival instinct. Sin is not just flawed evolution, or growing pains. It constitutes a broken relationship with God, and a radical departure from the good.

Nor is this just a Judeo-Christian insight. Many writers, from the ancient world on, have looked back to a lost 'golden age'—of Atlantis, or some other mythical kingdom. Eighteenth-century artists and writers looked back to the classical world as just such a golden age. Marxists look back to an age before inequality and private capital. Today's neo-Pagans look back to a day when humanity was one with the earth and idealize groups such as the Native Americans and Australians who seem to have clearer memories of that day than the rest of us. New Agers claim that there was once a holistic, more spiritual era before the arrival of western rationalism. Some radical feminists suggest there was a time before patriarchy, where the contributions of the feminine held sway. And revisionist theologians (those who challenge and want to revise traditional theological positions) look back to a supposed golden period before Augustine and the doctrine of original sin! It seems that something in our very bones tells us not only that there is something wrong with the world—but that there was a time *before* things went wrong. This awareness gives all these groups both a yardstick for seeing how far we have fallen, and a vision for change in the present. To the Christian, this should all sound very familiar.

A revisionist theology also deals a death blow to the biblical claim that Jesus Christ came to bring healing and restoration from sin—not only for human beings, but for the whole cosmos. If the cosmos is simply the way it has always been and is supposed to be, then it doesn't need to be liberated from any kind of captivity to an alien bondage and decay (as Romans 8:19–22 appears to claim). These things are just normal. Human salvation becomes a variation on self-acceptance. Jesus becomes little more than a good moral example—although why we should admire his moral code of love and self-denial in a world which his Father created to be 'red in tooth and claw' is far from obvious.

Jack Spong states unequivocally that the death of Jesus was in no sense a sacrifice for sin. He suggests, instead, that each person has to find their own understanding of how Jesus might—in some personal way—help him. For himself, he finds that Jesus calls him 'to live, to love, and to be'. More specifically, Jesus gives him 'the courage to be myself' (p. 243). But these are the clichés of the therapist's couch or the shampoo ad, the platitudes of a therapeutic culture obsessed with the self and its unfettered potential. They hardly match up to the majestic and devastating language of sin and salvation we encountered in the last chapter. This certainly isn't the awe-inspiring, heart-stopping message that converted the Roman Empire and provoked tears and screams in Puritan New England.

Spong's approach is to take what he and the chattering classes of his day happen to find intellectually acceptable, and to rewrite the faith accordingly. It is all rather reminiscent of the monstrous innkeeper from the Greek legends of Theseus, who decided that it was his bed that was the right size, and his guests who were the wrong size—so he chopped off any human limbs that didn't fit into his bed. The revisionist chops theology to fit the prejudices and preconceptions of his own day. He rules out *a priori* that God might have revealed definitive truths about himself and human nature in the history of Israel, the person of Jesus and the experiences of the New Testament writers. And he rules out *a priori* the possibility that his own whole worldview could be deficient.

The chopping of the revisionists also produces an anaemic version of the faith. The historic picture of a Jesus who died for the sin of the world might well provoke gratitude, ecstasy and personal and corporate up-heaval. But the revisionist Jesus who calls people to 'be themselves' might (at best) evoke an appreciative, 'Thank you. I shall certainly try to be myself.' It is hardly the stuff of changed lives and changed societies. It looks suspiciously like a sprinkle of positive thinking for complacent, self-satisfied Westerners.

One evening in May 1738, John Wesley attended a Moravian Christian meeting in Aldersgate Street, London. While there, he experi-enced a profound encounter with the majesty and self-sacrificial love of God. He later wrote, 'I felt my heart strangely warmed.' The revisionist theologian replaces this with a God who is a big, huggy teddy bear. And all he can say of this encounter is, 'I felt my cultural preconceptions strangely massaged.'

The revisionist programme seems to be a horrendous case of throwing out the baby with the bath water. The radical, revisionist theologians have elevated the fashionable ideas of their day to a position of ultimate authority. They have consequently asked Adam to leave the house quietly and close the door after him. Little did they realize that with him would go Jesus, and the goodness of God. And at the same time, they are throwing out much of their basis for working to combat cruelty and injustice.

Augustine and original sin

The Christian Church has always preserved the biblical revelation of the goodness of God, and has laid the blame for evil in the world on some sort of rebellion within the creation. It has always separated the origins of good in the universe from the origins of evil. The traditional phrase used to express this rebellion is 'original sin'. Christians believe that the doctrine of original sin has roots in the Bible, but its classic expression was formulated in the fourth and early fifth centuries by Augustine, a bishop in North Africa and a prolific writer of books and popular songs. Down the years, Christians have debated the finer points of the doctrine, but have agreed on its essential characteristics. Original sin is universal and unavoidable, and it is 'Adamic'.

Universal and unavoidable

Everybody, everywhere, has fallen out of relationship with God, and fallen short of his moral holiness. All areas of human life—and the whole creation—are affected by human rebellion in some way. Even people in the remotest tribes are tainted by original sin. And original sin taints our human nature from birth. No matter how well brought up a child might be, or how hard we try in adulthood, original sin will always make its presence felt in our fallen human nature.

The biblical basis for the view that original sin is universal and unavoidable lies in a range of passages such as those already mentioned in the last chapter: 'All have sinned and fall short of the glory of God' (Romans 3:23); 'There is none righteous, not even one' (Romans 3:10); 'Who can say, "I have kept my heart pure; I am clean and without sin"?' (Proverbs 20:9); 'All have turned aside, they have together become corrupt; there is no one who does good, not even one' (Psalm 14:3); 'If we claim to be without sin, we deceive ourselves and the truth is not in us' (1 John 1:8); 'If any of you is without sin, let him be the first to throw a stone' (John 8:7).

'Adamic'

Sin is not simply an eternal, paradoxical truth about human nature—that we evolved to be somehow, inexplicably, a mix of good and bad. Sin had a historical origin separate from the origins of goodness and the origins of the cosmos. The disobedience of Adam and Eve started something whose effects are still profoundly real. Like it or not, we are implicated in something bigger than ourselves, and that something can be traced back to Eden.

The main biblical basis for tracing original sin back to Adam lies in a combination of the early part of Genesis and Paul's letter to the Romans, particularly its fifth chapter. There is also good evidence that this was a belief Jesus himself shared. We shall look briefly at each of these passages.

In Genesis 2 and 3, Adam is presented both as an individual man, and in some sense a representative man (*Adam*, as we have seen, means 'mankind'). In Romans, similarly, Paul writes of Adam in terms that clearly show he believed he was a real person. His parallels between Adam and Jesus strongly imply that Adam was every bit as real as Jesus. But Paul also writes of Adam as a kind of covenant head, or representative, of all humanity. Paul repeatedly emphasizes both points: 'Sin entered the world through one man' (Romans 5:12); 'If the many died by the trespass of the one man, how much more did God's grace and the gift that came by the grace of the one man, Jesus Christ, overflow to the many!' (5:15); 'Consequently, just as the result of one trespass was condemnation for all men, so also the result of one act of righteousness was justification that brings life for all men. For just as through the disobedience of the one man the many were made sinners, so also through the obedience of the one man the many will be made righteous' (5:18–19). The same Adam–Jesus parallels are drawn in 1 Corinthians 15:22: 'For as in Adam all die, so in Christ all will be made alive.'

It is sometimes claimed that Jesus himself says nothing about original sin, or about the role of Adam in originating it, and that he simply assumes the present reality of sinfulness and the need for repentance. It is certainly true that Jesus assumes the fact of sin. But it is not strictly true that he ignores the place of Adam, a fact which is particularly clear in his teaching on marriage (Matthew 19). When a group of Pharisees ask Jesus about divorce, Jesus' reply is telling. He says, 'Moses permitted you to divorce your wives because your hearts were hard. But *it was not this way from the beginning*' (Matthew 19:8). In the parallel passage in Mark 10, the reference is more explicit, referring back to God's original creation of Adam and Eve. There are strong grounds for believing that Jesus assumes something drastic must have gone wrong after the first two chapters of Genesis—something that messed up relationships, hardened hearts and necessitated a whole new approach to law and morality. There was a fall.

But is original sin credible?

The idea of original sin has clear attractions. It does justice to the biblical material on sin. It retains a central, awe-inspiring place for Jesus Christ as God's solution to sin. It upholds the absolute goodness of God. It preserves the hard-hitting and radical claims of the gospel against the bland, introspective psycho-speak of some revisionist theologians.

But a lingering doubt remains in the minds of many. The idea of a fall may be theologically neat and morally helpful, but is it really credible? Can a thinking person today seriously believe all that stuff about Adam and Eve, particularly given the insights of evolutionary science? Here is the reason many find the arguments of the anti-fall revisionists so convincing. It is not so much that people want to deny the reality of human fallenness: they can see that with their eyes. They just find it impossible to believe in the Genesis account as actual history, and can't quite believe that anybody else might see it as more than a story. Most are happy to accept some idea of present *fallenness*. Where they hesitate is over a historic *fall*.

Yet, as we have found, any account of human nature and the condition of the world which denies that any kind of space–time fall occurred runs into problems, both moral and theological. And there does seem something inconsistent, even dishonest, about those theologians who want to keep the benefits of saying that human beings are *fallen*, without admitting that human beings actually *fell*. This desire to keep the meaning without the event feels rather like claiming that somebody is legally married without ever having had a marriage ceremony, or that somebody is dead without having died. To say that our fallen nature has always been that way, as long as people have existed, is, surely, to do away with categories of 'fallenness' altogether. It is to say that God made us this way and (presumably) wants us to stay this way.

So is there any way of simultaneously holding on to Christian orthodoxy about the fall, and not sacrificing our minds? Is it possible to formulate an intelligent account of the faith that does justice both to the biblical account and to the best insights of contemporary science?

Some theologians and atheistic scientists, such as Oxford biologist Richard Dawkins, express cynicism. But orthodox Christian thinkers have always insisted not only that this is possible, but that good theology and good science always belong together. We shall spend the rest of this chapter exploring the main options by which contemporary Christian thinkers have attempted to bring together all the relevant data. In each case, we shall look at how the advocates of this particular view handle both the biblical material and scientific issues. This will involve temporarily moving away from a direct focus on our theme of sin, but it is all necessary background for clear thinking about the origins of sin.

Remember, we have already rejected the view that the fall has no historical basis at all. All the following accounts of the entry of sin into the world assume that things have not always been the way they are now. Somewhere along the line, something went very wrong.

Literal–Universal fall

This view of the fall takes a fairly literal approach to the biblical material, and rejects the theory of evolution as incompatible with it. Since the early 20th century, the main defenders of this position have been known as 'creationists' due to their belief in a literal, six-day creation. More recently, however, the cause has been boosted by some high-calibre thinkers who have brought a new level of sophistication to the Christian anti-evolutionary case. First, we review the traditional creationist arguments.

In terms of the Bible, creationists insist that scripture is not only God-breathed (2 Timothy 3:16), but absolutely inerrant in all it teaches. One of the ablest defenders of a creationist position is Dr Henry M. Morris, of the Institute for Creation Research in San Diego, California. In his book *Evolution and the Modern Christian* (Presbyterian & Reformed, 1967), Morris claims that 'the Biblical record of origins was written to be understood and therefore is to be taken literally rather than mystically or parabolically' (p. 55). He states that the early part of Genesis should not be described as allegory, hymn or myth. To do so, he says, would be to undermine the authority of the rest of the Bible too:

If the early chapters of Genesis are not historical and correct, there is no escaping the conclusion that Paul and Peter and the other writers of the New Testament were guilty of either ignorance or misrepresentation when they cited these events as true and as, in fact, foundational in the entire plan of salvation. (p. 57)

For Morris, the whole of Genesis is a historical account. God created the world in six days, and all creatures by special acts of creation. Adam and Eve were two real individuals who were tempted by Satan in the form of a real serpent. The result was a fall from the fellowship with God that they had once enjoyed. This fall then extended out into the natural world, accounting for the existence of struggle and death in nature. The scriptural basis for this lies in Genesis 3:17: 'Cursed is the ground because of you…'. In that sense the creationist believes in not only a literal but also a *universal* fall, involving humanity and the rest of nature alike.

Morris believes that the 'death' that came into the world through the sin of Adam (Genesis 3:3; Romans 5:12–19) involves not only spiritual death but actual, physical death too. Prior to the fall, death was alien to God's good creation. Of course, Adam and Eve do not physically die the moment they taste the fruit. Rather, it is that *mortality* is introduced into the creation. God tells Adam he must now work 'until you return to the ground, since from it you were taken; for dust you are and to dust you will return' (Genesis 3:19). This reading is supported by Paul in 1 Corinthians 15:22: 'For as in Adam all die, so in Christ all will be made alive.' In context, this has to be a reference to physical mortality—Paul's whole chapter is about physical death and bodily resurrection.

This inerrantist view of the Bible is coupled with a scepticism about evolutionary theory. The main reasons put forward for this are biblical. Genesis says that God sees his handiwork as perfect and complete: 'God saw all that he had made, and it was very good' (Genesis 1:31). This, say the creationists, means that God's manner of creating did not include struggle, predation (creatures acting in a predatory manner), or death. Furthermore, God created each species 'after its kind' (Genesis 1:11–25), which precludes variation from one animal type to another. Creationists argue their case from science too. Morris and his colleagues have consistently stood against the evolutionary consensus among most biologists and paleontologists, claiming that the scientific evidence does not support evolution.

The creationists' scientific case against evolution has traditionally taken a number of lines of attack. First, they admit that biological mutations do occur and are observable, but these are always micro-mutations, from one variety to another. There is no evidence, they claim, that macro-mutations could happen, which would change one 'kind' of creature into another. Second, the fossil record shows no intermediate stages from the mutation of one kind of animal into another; all forms of animal life appear quite suddenly, and fully formed. The transitional forms we might expect if evolution were true simply aren't there, they say. Third, creationists have argued that evolution contradicts the Second Law of Thermodynamics, or entropy, which states that the universe is moving irrevocably in the direction of disorder, disintegration and decay. Evolution, on the other hand, has to claim that there is a universal tendency for life forms to become more complex and adapted.

Theological support for the creationist cause has come mostly from the ranks of American 'inerrantists', notably Francis Schaeffer's *Genesis in Space and Time* (IVP, 1972). Until the early 1990s, the creationists and their theological supporters fought a lonely battle, shunned by theologians who took a less literal view of Genesis, lampooned by the scientific establishment, and stereotyped as ignorant hicks in the media. But the Christian anti-evolutionary case received a substantial shot in the arm during the 1990s, with sophisticated contributions from a law professor and a leading biochemist.

Berkeley law professor Phillip Johnson is a specialist in the logic of arguments. During a 1987 sabbatical in the UK, he bought a number of books on Darwinian evolution and was intrigued to see how weak he found the evidence they contained. He came to the conclusion that Darwinism had found such widespread acceptance not for reasons of pure science (as most people assume), but because it gave intellectual credibility to a whole way of looking at the world. Darwinism offers a coherent account of origins without any need for God. In the words of biologist Richard Dawkins, Darwin 'made it possible to be an intellectually fulfilled atheist' (*The Blind Watchmaker*, Longman, 1986, p. 6).

In books such as *Darwin on Trial* (IVP USA, 1991; UK edition Monarch, 1994), *Reason in the Balance* (IVP, 1995), and *Wedge of Truth* (IVP, 2000), Johnson carefully reframed the terms of the debate. The real battle, he said, is not between evolution and creation. It is between 'naturalism' and intelligent design. By naturalism, Johnson means an atheistic worldview which holds that natural causes alone can explain everything. In *Darwin on Trial*, Johnson also casts a critical lawyer's eye over the evidence for evolution and finds it singularly lacking, in areas such as the mutation of species and the fossil record. Johnson accuses evolutionists of a prior commitment to the philosophy of naturalism, a religious belief that has not itself been demonstrated scientifically—and never could be.

Whatever one thinks of his anti-evolutionary stance, here Johnson surely has a point. It is not hard to find examples of a faith-commitment to naturalism smuggled in under the guise of hard science. Many science textbooks, and exhibits in museums of natural history, frequently include blatant propaganda for the worldview of naturalism, mixed in among the real science. The book of the BBC TV series *Ape Man: The Story of Human Evolution* (BBC, 2000), by Robin McKie, makes for a fascinating read but contains a few very unscientific assertions about humankind. In his Preface, McKie addresses the traditional view that human beings are a special, exalted creature. He curtly replies, 'We are nothing of the kind, of course' (p. 6). And he observes that 'good fortune, not predestined greatness, has been the leitmotif of the story of *Homo sapiens*' (p. 187). But such statements go beyond anything science is remotely qualified to comment on. Scientists may well claim to have traced a possible ancestry for humankind, but to conclude from this that we are not special in any way, or that evolution (if it happened) could not have been guided by an intelligent mind, go beyond any kind of empirical evidence. Such claims are devotional statements, from the pseudo-religion of naturalism.

Irrespective of one's position on the truth of evolution, it is undeniable that evolution (according to philosopher Mary Midgley) is the 'creation myth of our age'. In the popular mind, evolution is perceived as displacing the need for a religious explanation of life and origins. For most of the 19th and 20th centuries, evolution (in the words of an essay by C.S. Lewis) became the 'great Myth'. Writers such as H.G. Wells and George Bernard Shaw saw evolution as the key which explained practically everything, from human nature and society to art and morality. Some of this attitude still lingers. In an age that no longer believes in divine providence, evolution seems an appealing substitute.

While Phillip Johnson was touring university campuses, challenging evolutionists to reassess the logic of their case, another attack on Darwin's theory was emerging in the field of biochemistry. In his 1996 book *Darwin's Black Box: The Biochemical Challenge to Evolution* (Touchstone, 1996), biochemist Michael Behe develops the scientific idea of 'irreducible complexity'. An irreducibly complex organism is one made up of a number of interacting parts, the removal of any one of which would cause the whole system to stop functioning. Behe's favourite example of this is a mousetrap. All parts of the trap are needed to catch a mouse. It is not possible to catch a few mice with just a platform, a few more when you add a spring, and so on. To catch any mice at all, the whole trap must be assembled and all parts working. The mousetrap is irreducibly complex.

Behe points out how many living structures, such as cells, are like the mousetrap—irreducibly complex. A cell is not so much a single structure as a whole factory of interlinked structures. If one part of the system were to evolve apart from the others, the whole system couldn't begin to work. But Darwinian natural selection has to assume that this is precisely how species did evolve: by countless minor mutations, over a long period of time. But the evidence of the natural world shows that most mutations are harmful and, according to the logic of Darwinism itself, make an organism *less* adapted to its environment. When organisms form an integrated whole, a mutation is not progress: it is a potentially lethal disruption of the harmonious working of the whole.

Behe claims that Darwinism cannot account for the origins of irreducibly complex structures in the first place, or for the ongoing mutation of one irreducibly complex life form into another. Using his mousetrap analogy, Behe concludes that a more reasonable account of irreducible complexity is given by the idea of intelligent design. If scientists reject the idea of a creator, says Behe (echoing Phillip Johnson), it is less from studying the evidence than from a prior religious–philosophical commitment to naturalism.

Johnson and Behe, and a growing body of scientists who also question orthodox Darwinism, have reframed the Christian debate over origins, making the old stereotype of anti-evolutionists as uneducated fundamentalists harder to sustain. These are intellectuals, who have moved away from the old creationist–evolutionist polarization, to a more sophisticated pitting of blind naturalism against intelligent design. Which, they ask, best fits the empirical evidence? At the same time, these 'new creationists' bracket out some of the less easily defended claims of the older creationists, such as their theory that the earth is not billions of years old, but only thousands. They focus their energies on one central thesis: that the irreducible complexity of life on earth is better accounted for by the hypothesis of an intelligent designer than of blind, unguided evolution.

Nevertheless, the new creationists can still be categorized alongside the older creationists for present purposes, in that they too tend to deny that evolution is compatible with Christian faith. From this camp emerges an understanding of the fall as literal (the first three chapters of Genesis form a reasonably straightforward historical account), and universal (humanity fell from innocence into sin, which introduced death and suffering into a previously pristine creation).

The case is well argued by Charles Colson in his major book on shaping a Christian worldview, *How Now Shall We Live?* (Tyndale, 1999). Colson, a former Nixon White House aide-turned-Christian statesman, points out that our theories of origins and the historicity of the fall have massive repercussions across areas such as ethics, the legal system and the arts. He claims that Darwin was a man committed to a philosophy of naturalism, which he then sought to justify scientifically.

Colson states bluntly, 'Many Christians shrink from drawing such a stark contrast between theism and Darwinism. They hope to combine Darwin's biological theory with belief in God—suggesting that God may have used evolution as his method of creating. Yet Darwin himself insisted that the two are mutually exclusive' (p. 94). Colson later adds, 'We must be clear what is at stake here. As long as Darwinism reigns in our schools and élite culture, the Christian worldview will be considered the madwoman in the attic—irrational and unbelievable. That's why we can no longer allow naturalists to treat science as a sanctuary where their personal philosophy reigns free from challenge' (p. 97).

Symbolic–Universal fall

This second view also believes in a historic fall that was universal in scope, affecting human beings and the natural world alike. But its approach to both the relevant biblical and scientific material is quite different. For those who hold this view, the early chapters of Genesis are to be read symbolically rather than literally, and its advocates are more open to the insights of contemporary science, particularly evolutionary theory.

First, let's consider their use of scripture. The approach of this group of Christian thinkers to the opening chapters of Genesis is well summarized by the eminent French Reformed theologian, Henri Blocher. In his study *Original Sin* (Apollos, 1997), he makes a vital distinction: 'The real issue when we try to interpret Genesis 2—3 is not whether we have a historical account of the fall, but whether or not we may read it as the account of a historical fall' (p. 50). This is a distinction not made in the Literal–Universal view above, which assumes that to safeguard the historicity of the fall, Genesis must be written as what readers today would recognize as history. But this, say advocates of a Symbolic–Universal fall, is an unsound assumption, which imposes our own categories on to the biblical material.

Instead, supporters of the Symbolic–Universal view insist that the material itself invites a less literalistic reading. For one, the events recounted could not possibly have been an eye-witness account. What we appear to have is an artistic, literary account of origins—written long after the event, in highly symbolic and stylized language. It is an account accessible to the human imagination, a story that still grips readers millennia after it was written. Symbolic trees, a talking snake, God making Adam from the clay and breathing life into him, God creating woman from the man's rib, flaming angelic swords: these are recognizably the language of ancient myth and saga. The narrative of the serpent tempting the couple to aspire to forbidden, godlike knowledge finds an obvious echo in the Greek myth of Prometheus, stealing from the gods the fire which they had withheld from humankind.

This 'mythological' aspect of Genesis remains true even if we believe that the account of Eden is a divinely inspired, factual, or 'archetypal' myth. And it remains true if, as many theologians point out, the dissimilarities with ancient sagas are even more striking (the two trees and the fruit that leads to death are unique to Genesis; most ancient myths portray serpents as divine helpers, but the Genesis serpent embodies rebellion and death; unlike the Greek gods in the Prometheus story, God withholds something to test the couple, not to deny them something good; and so forth).

God himself is portrayed in terms that humans can relate to.

Although God is beyond human imagining, and God is spirit, he 'walks' in the garden; he is presented as a gardener, surgeon, worker with clay and tailor. Names too are highly symbolic: Adam is Hebrew for 'man' or 'humankind' in a generic sense, as well as the name of an individual. The name Eve evokes the Hebrew for 'living'. Abel means both 'breath' and 'temporary', highlighting the brevity of his life. None of this need imply that the events retold are in any sense less than true, or less than inspired. The debate is over what *kind* of inspired writing we find in Genesis 2—3, and the text itself invites us not to impose on it modern-day categories of what counts as history.

We can summarize all this as follows. The early part of Genesis tells of a rupture in the relationship between humankind and God. This was a real event, which happened in time and space, with universal implications. But our account of this fall, though it happened in history, could not possibly be told within the terms of normal historical writing. Instead, it is told in the language of saga or parable, a language well suited to retelling history in a way which is universally accessible and which grips the imagination.

In terms of science, supporters of a Symbolic–Universal position tend to be sympathetic towards mainstream evolutionary theory, not seeing it as incompatible *per se* with biblical faith. Two main groups insist that Darwinist evolution and Christian faith are mutually exclusive: secularists, and those Christians who hold to the literal view of Genesis 2—3. Not so, say those who take a more symbolic view of Genesis.

Nor is it safe to assume that these people are necessarily theological liberals. One of Darwin's early supporters was the American Calvinist B.B. Warfield, a fierce proponent of biblical inerrancy. So were a number of other prominent evangelicals of the day, such as James McCosh, President of Princeton University. The origins of the term 'fundamentalism' date back to a series of booklets published between 1910 and 1915 in the UK and USA, on the 'fundamentals' of faith. One of the contributors was Warfield. Another was Scottish theologian James Orr, who also saw no conflict between the Bible and current scientific discoveries, including evolution. Another was geologist George Wright, who even believed that evolution, if proved, would strengthen rather than weaken the argument that the earth is the product of intelligent design. Clearly, the early fundamentalists were far from self-evidently anti-evolution! The views of Orr and Warfield were also close to the official Roman Catholic position of the day.

How did these Christian thinkers come to their conclusion that far from being antagonistic to faith, mainstream science could actually help our understanding of the Bible? There is a strong tradition in the Christian Church which holds that God reveals himself in two 'books' —the Bible and nature. In one, we have a specific revelation of salvation, in the other a general revelation of God's creative power and moral character. This accords well with what might be called the Bible's own 'natural theology'. The psalmist sees the natural world as revealing God, because it is God's own creation (Psalm 8:3; 19:1; 102:25 and so on). And the apostle Paul insists that God's existence and his character are evident to all people, everywhere, from study of the created world (Romans 1:20).

Princeton theologian Charles Hodge, a traditionalist in matters of theology, wrote in 1863, 'Nature is as truly a revelation of God as the Bible; and we only interpret the Word of God by the Word of God when we interpret the Bible by science.' His Princeton colleague James McCosh made a similar point: 'When a scientific theory is brought before us, our enquiry is not whether it is consistent with religion, but whether it is true.' In other words, there is a distinguished tradition of biblical theology which takes with utmost seriousness both the revelation of scripture and the witness of scientific discovery. Both offer vital insights into the nature of God, and each should be understood as shedding light on the other. If one appears to contradict the other, then we need to ask ourselves whether our current understanding of either scripture or science is adequate. The discovery of God's truth has to emerge from an ongoing, creative dialogue between the Bible and scientific discovery.

What does this do to a reading of Genesis 2—3? It means that we must listen to the 'book' of evolutionary science, and not prejudge that evolutionists are by definition supporters of atheistic naturalism. Some· undoubtedly are. But many are practising Christians (even, in some cases, 'fundamentalists'), with a high view of the authority of the Bible. We cannot now go into all the reasons why most scientists remain convinced that evolution happened, and that the mechanisms by which it happened were well described by Darwin. A useful summary is offered from a Christian perspective by R.J. Berry, in his books *God and Evolution* (Hodder, 1988), and *God and the Biologist* (IVP, 1996). Suffice to say, most scientists find the evidence compelling, even those with a deep Christian commitment. Nevertheless, it is clearly relevant to review current research on human origins.

At the time of writing, the broad consensus among mainstream scientists on human evolution goes something like this. Human beings (*Homo sapiens*) share a common biological ancestry with species of apes (98 per cent of the DNA in our bodies is shared with chimpanzees). Around five or six million years ago, two separate lines emerged—one leading to humankind, the other to chimpanzees. The line that eventually led to us was not a simple linear progression, but more like a tree or bush, with different branches. From around two million to about 300,000 years ago, many different hominid forms coexisted. Most of these cannot be described as 'pre-human', as they were not our ancestors: recent DNA tests on bones identified as Neanderthal show conclusively that they were not our ancestors. This coexistence of different hominid types is described by author Robin McKie in his book *Ape Man* as a 'Star Wars bar', after the scene in the sci-fi film where a range of aliens all drink and talk together!

Our own species, *Homo sapiens*, appears first to have emerged around 200,000 years ago, in the Paleolithic era (or 'Old Stone Age'). Evidence from paleontologists points to the origins of *Homo sapiens* in East Africa during this period, and many DNA researchers are confident that all humans can trace their ancestry back to a single African woman, a so-called 'African Eve'. Next, there is strong evidence that around 40,000 years ago, there was a significant cultural leap forward among *Homo sapiens*. From this time on, we have strong evidence for artwork of great sophistication (such as cave paintings and ivory carvings), music and cultural life, including ritual and religion, and evidence of reflective thought. Another massive cultural advance took place around 10,000 years ago, the early days of the Neolithic era (or 'New Stone Age').

This was the point when societies in Mesopotamia (the land between the Euphrates and Tigris rivers in modern-day Iraq) and the Jordan Valley shifted from hunting and foraging to agriculture and stock-rearing, and developed a more sophisticated use of stone and flint. These practices then spread rapidly through both Turkey and the Nile Valley, leading in turn to the rise of settled communities and—in time—the first cities and literate civilizations.

All this evidence about our origins seems to fit quite happily with a symbolic view of Genesis 2—3. God's chosen method of creation was over long periods of time, rather than in six literal days. What about Adam and Eve? One option is that they lived in East Africa, around 200,000 years ago, and were the true progenitors of the race. Although this couple had hominid ancestry, God deliberately chose to imprint the new *Homo sapiens* with his image in a new and unique way. The divine breath breathed into them set them apart from all hominid forms that had gone before. The moment they turned away from God, sin and death entered the world and infected the whole creation, non-human as well as human.

In this scenario, the 'death' that came into the world through the sin of Adam (see Genesis 3:3; Romans 5:12–19) was neither immediate physical death nor mortality, but separation from God, who is the source of all life. It is exclusion from eternal life. This is the sense in which the word is used in the letter to the Ephesians: 'As for you, you were dead in your transgressions and sins' (2:1). The fall, then, marks the origins of separation from God, which is also called sin. But this is not the same as mortality, which already existed. (Interestingly, this is the exact opposite of the view of many Jewish theologians, who hold that the 'death' that came into the world through Adam was only physical mortality, and not spiritual death.)

In this version of the Symbolic–Universal view of the fall, Adam and Eve are Africans, living around 200,000 years ago. They are a chosen and special primal couple who choose to reject God's design for them. The result is a fall, which is inherited by all subsequent generations of the whole human race, and the effects of this fall then ripple out into the whole creation in various ways. The result is a new, damaged nature which already included death, but now includes suffering, illness, predatory behaviour and natural disasters.

Around 200,000 years ago, something profound happened which affected the whole created order. This involves reading not only Genesis 2—3 as symbolic. Genesis 4—11 (from Cain through to the flood) must also be read not so much as a family genealogy as a digest, or précis, of thousands of years of history (or, rather, pre-history), highlighting the main players, until we arrive at a more datable kind of history with Abraham from chapter 12 onwards.

Symbolic–Spiritual fall

A third view of the fall is essentially a variation on the Symbolic–Universal position just outlined, as is a fourth option which we shall consider in a moment. Some Christian evolutionists see a weakness in the scenario just outlined. Their dilemma can be summarized in a short sentence: dinosaurs got arthritis! These critics question the traditional assumption that when the parents of *Homo sapiens* fell, at that moment the rest of nature fell with them. Instead, they point to evidence that there was not only death, but also illness, suffering and predation in nature millions of years ago. Certainly, these things appear on the face of it to have existed long before the arrival of human beings.

This third position, and the fourth which we are about to consider, both represent possible ways of accounting for this. The present option affirms the historicity of Adam and Eve and the fall, but denies that they were biological parents of the whole human race, and denies that their fall brought any kind of substantial damage to the natural world. The fall was essentially a spiritual affair, restricted to human nature.

In this scenario, the couple might have lived much later than the first arrival of *Homo sapiens*, 200,000 years ago. One possible setting could have been the start of the explosion of culture and the arts around 40,000 years ago. This could have been the result of God breathing a new dimension of divine life into Adam and Eve, and new skills spread rapidly through human cultures. At that stage of history,

Homo sapiens had already settled across much of the globe. Adam and Eve would then be not so much the genetic parents of the race, but a couple selected by God, from among other *Homo sapiens*, to have a new and unique covenant relationship with himself, just as later in Genesis God chooses Abraham from all the people on earth. This couple in a special sense become representative of all humanity, who are all implicated in Adam's sin, despite being separated from Adam in space or time.

This account is biblically plausible. When the unity of humankind 'in Adam' is discussed in the New Testament, there is no clear insistence that we inherit sin biologically. Rather, Adam appears to be seen more as a representative, covenant head of humanity before God. We are held to be spiritually united under his 'headship'. We shall explore this issue of how sin is transmitted in greater detail in the next chapter.

The Professor of Genetics at University College, London, R.J. Berry, favours a solution along these lines, but dates it during the later cultural explosion. He holds that God created Adam in the body of a farmer, living in ancient Mesopotamia some 10,000 years ago. This would place him at the preliminary stages of the Neolithic period, at the point where *Homo sapiens* developed crop-growing and stock-rearing. Adam and Eve were not literally the first man and woman, but the first to be filled with the breath of God in a new and different way, the first to be made in God's image.

This, he says, fits the picture of agrarian life presented in Genesis 2 and 3, and details such as the 'cool of the evening' in Genesis 3:8 (the high plateau around the upper reaches of the River Tigris would have cool evenings). This would also fit the ancient Sumerian location for Eden, and explain old chestnuts such as where Cain got his wife from, and who the mysterious Nephilim were (Genesis 6:4). Berry points out that Genesis 4, with its descriptions of the different types of farming, makes for a fair summary of Neolithic culture. This Adam and Eve then turn from God and fall spiritually. Their representative function means that this fall becomes the spiritual fall of all humanity.

Berry addresses the thorny question of how dinosaurs could have got arthritis before the fall, by warning against Christian speculation on life before the fall. In *God and the Biologist*, he chides some believers for their tendency to blame anything they find morally difficult, such as predatory behaviour among animals, and miscarriage in pregnancy, as 'results of the fall'. Perhaps, says Berry, part of our problem is that we anthropomorphize (read human characteristics into) the animal world, seeing predation on a par with human killing, and assume that experiences such as miscarriage are necessarily bad. His suggestion is that such characteristics of the natural world may simply be a 'normal' part of God's creation, and that the real problem is our assumption that such things must have been caused by the fall.

How, then, does Berry handle biblical passages such as Romans 8:20–22, which talks about the creation being 'subjected to frustration', in 'bondage to decay', and 'groaning as in the pains of childbirth'? Don't these imply that the earth was once perfect, and sin introduced distortion in nature?

He suggests, in *God and the Biologist*, that such references need to be read in the following context. The fall resulted not in physical death but in separation from God. This, in turn, led to a distortion in the relationship between the man and the woman (Genesis 3:16; 4:7), and between humankind and the natural world. The 'tending' in Eden becomes 'toil' outside (Genesis 3:18). It is the second of these broken relationships which is relevant here. The 'frustration' of the natural world (which literally means 'futility' or 'purposelessness') results from humanity failing to tend and care for it as God had intended, as God's managers on earth.

In this scenario, the broad sweep of the argument in Romans 8:18–23 is therefore about human environmental responsibility, saying that salvation in Christ can redeem this aspect of the fall too. Paul is saying that as long as we are bound by sin—the effect of the fall—we fail in our call to be stewards of creation. But salvation restores the relationship with nature which sin broke. The message of hope in these verses, then, is not *eschatological*—looking forward to the new heaven and new earth as the day when the effects of the fall on nature are undone. Instead, it is *ecological*—concerning the moment when people's relationship with God is restored in Christ, and we begin to live out the consequences of this for a restored relationship with nature too. At that point, believers will take up our intended role as managers and stewards of creation.

So Berry does not deny that the fall affects the natural world in some way. It does. But this is not the traditional view that the human fall rippled out into creation, introducing alien practices such as predatory behaviour, illness and natural disasters. These things, he insists, were already there. Rather, Berry says that one of the relationships damaged by the fall was that between humanity and environment. Without the gardener, nature becomes wild and directionless—like an old, neglected garden. With a gardener back in post, it once again begins to regain its beauty and purposeful character.

Symbolic–Two Stage fall

This fourth view of the fall, like the two just outlined, assumes an evolutionary framework. And, like the Symbolic–Spiritual position, it represents a way of explaining how suffering could have occurred in the natural world before the creation and fall of humankind. The Symbolic–Spiritual option concluded that the fall was a purely spiritual affair, affecting only human nature, and that acts such as predatory killing or illness may in fact just be a normal part of God's creation. It claimed that the problem is our labelling such actions as 'bad', rather than the actions in themselves. This view of the fall gives a coherent account of how pre-fall 'imperfections' existed in creation, by redefining our assumptions about the nature of the fall, and about what life before the fall might have been like.

Nevertheless, some Christians are instinctively unhappy with this solution. It mostly reduces the scope of the fall to human beings, and invites us to rethink what we currently see as evidence of evil or 'fallenness' in the natural world. It says that maybe these aspects of nature, from which we recoil, are simply part of the God-given order of things. The problem with this position, for some people, is that they simply cannot accept the picture it presents of the pre-fall world. It implies that God's original, perfect natural order includes killing other creatures for one's own survival. Pain is enshrined not simply as an unwelcome intruder in the world, but as God's planned way of the world. God, in other words, has blood on his hands.

This begins to look like a milder variation on the position we rejected at the start of this chapter: that there was no historic fall. True, the Berry position (unlike the more liberal approaches) keeps a historic fall of mankind. And it ties this fall in to the well-being of the natural world. It also retains our need for a saviour. But if we pursue the ethical implications of his position, some people feel that things become rather unsettling. If it is true that God designed a world where predatory behaviour is good and normal, do we then have a strong basis for caring for animals ourselves? Is it just anthropomorphic sentiment to squirm at seeing a lion ripping a gazelle apart, or even a cat killing a bird in the garden? If so, might it not equally be anthropomorphic sentiment to object to inhumane farming methods, my drunken neighbour kicking his dog, or small boys pulling the legs off insects?

And if the God-given natural order is of natural selection, or survival of the fittest—which Berry, a Christian Darwinist, believes in—it also becomes harder to justify fighting for the rights of disabled people, or the unborn, or to help famine victims in already overpopulated areas of the world.

Historic Christian theology has always found this sort of position inadequate. The natural world is not simply a more or less neutral backdrop, against which a purely human drama of sin and salvation is played out. Nature is itself fallen. This was clearly enshrined in our first two accounts of evolution and the fall—creationism, and the evolutionary scenario with Adam and Eve as literal first parents of the race. But we also found that both these options failed to account for how disaster, disease and predation could have existed millions of years ago, as the 'book' of nature strongly suggests they did. How did dinosaurs get arthritis, if disease only came in with the fall?

This fourth position, the Symbolic–Two Stage fall, answers that dilemma. It assumes the basically evolutionary framework underlying the two scenarios we have just explored, but goes on to say in effect that there were two falls—the first, in the pre-human cosmos and the natural world; the second, affecting humankind.

This is a position that has been gathering support among thinking Christians over the past century or so. One current advocate of it is the English theologian Michael Lloyd. Lloyd points out, in his essay 'The Humanity of Fallenness' from the essay collection *Grace and Truth in the Secular Age* (Eerdmans, 1998), that the Genesis account of the world before the fall is not in fact an unspoilt paradise. The world already contained a serpent who was acting contrary to God's will and tempting others to do the same. Second, the fact that the couple are called to 'subdue' the earth and 'rule over' the beasts (Genesis 1:28) implies that an element of disorder or rebellion already exists, needing to be brought into line. Third, Lloyd observes that while Genesis says the couple are in a fertile and co-operative garden, it nowhere says that this garden is the whole world, or that the whole world shares its *shalom*. In fact, this garden may be a restorative bridgehead in an already fallen natural world.

The most natural explanation for how the pre-human natural world came to be fallen draws on the Judeo-Christian tradition of an angelic fall, which somehow distorted the evolution of life on earth. Most Christians have always believed in some kind of fall of spiritual beings, including Satan, which predated the fall of human beings. But this Symbolic–Two Stage position takes things further by suggesting that this first fall affected the development of pre-human life on earth. This is a position held by a number of respected contemporary theologians, including Hans Urs von Balthasar, Alvin Plantinga, Eric Mascall and Stephen Davis, as well as C.S. Lewis, whose writings in the middle of the 20th century influenced many Christian thinkers. It is also the one I personally tend towards.

In this scenario, in the very beginning God created a good universe, which included spiritual beings who possessed a measure of free will. Satan and his angels rebelled, spreading a web of poison in God's perfect creation. So nature—following the fall of Satan and his angels, but before the creation of Adam and Eve—is not perfect. Dinosaurs get arthritis. Animals kill other animals. Pre-human hominids know what it is to hate and murder, and suffer from diseases.

The creation of humankind 'in the image of God' then becomes the first phase of God's rescue plan for the earth. Subsequent stages will include the covenant with Abraham and the coming of Jesus. Humankind is given a vocation to cooperate in God's healing purposes for the cosmos. But instead we join the rebellion. We go over to the dark side (to use the language of *Star Wars*).

This also sheds fresh light on the ministry of Jesus. Here, at last, is a man who responds to the human calling to resist the pull of the dark side. His divine nature sets him apart from other men and women caught up in the effects of the fall. Jesus brings healing to a suffering creation. What would be more natural than to see evidence of the healing of nature and human life in his ministry, and the battle against demonic forces raging at full strength? If Adam and Eve had fulfilled their own calling, creation might have been restored long before. As it was, it took God himself coming to earth as man to inaugurate the long-awaited healing of our battered creation.

This fourth option seems to do justice to all the relevant factors. It takes seriously both the book of scripture and the 'book' of nature, as read by contemporary science. It preserves the absolute goodness of God and a basic historicity to the fall. It accounts for the role of Satan and demonic forces in the biblical drama, and in the ongoing experience of the Church. It gives us a basis for working as caring stewards of creation, as well as calling people to repent of sin and turn to God. It helps explain why paleontologists find fossil remains of dinosaurs with arthritis, and of pre-human hominids who appear to have suffered from excruciating illnesses. It accounts plausibly for the existence of suffering before the fall in Eden.

The origins of sin

We have explored the issue of the origins of sin in some detail in this chapter. It has to be admitted, however, that the New Testament's main theologian, Paul, does not himself give much attention to the origins of sin and evil in his writings. He simply assumes its existence, linking it in some way to the fall of Adam.

But we are thinking creatures, who are right to have a healthy suspicion of mumbo-jumbo, particularly when dressed in the clothing of theology. It is important that our theology of origins is not some wild fantasy which is hard to square with either scripture or science. But in this chapter we have found that historic Christianity can account for the origins of sin in a way which is intellectually satisfying, and does justice to everyday experience. My own sense is that the fourth option probably achieves this best, but any of the above are legitimate ways of reconciling Genesis and science. Each reader will have to decide which they find most persuasive.

One thing is clear, however. We can hold open the books of scripture and nature, confident that both offer true revelations of the creator. There are clear signs that Christians are moving beyond the stale creation–evolution polarizations of the past. Christian evolutionists and anti-evolutionists alike are rallying round a shared position which holds that intelligent design explains the empirical evidence better than naturalism, as well as doing justice to the biblical revelation.

In Chapter 6, we shall finally explore in greater detail God's rescue plan for the cosmos. Before we do, we must take a closer look at one more facet of sin—how it is passed on. Adam sinned. But how did this sin affect me? Isn't it unfair to blame me for a sin I never committed? And what about the devil? Can we really still believe in a being with horns and a pointy tail, and does he still play any kind of role in this whole drama?

CHAPTER 5

Passing It On

'A boy!' said she. 'Do you mean you are a Son of Adam?'
Edmund stood still, saying nothing. He was too confused
by this time to understand what the question meant.

C.S. LEWIS, *THE LION, THE WITCH AND THE WARDROBE*

By a different name, about you the tale is told.

HORACE, *SATIRES*

In Adam

In this chapter we explore one of the main riddles of sin—how it is transmitted. More specifically, we shall look at how the sin of Adam can be said to affect each one of us, and precisely what is transmitted from Adam to the rest of humanity. Then we shall take a look at whether our natural human sinfulness is due to a purely human rebellion, or whether there might also be some other spiritual power pulling us in the wrong direction. First, how sin is passed on, and just what it is that we receive from Adam.

If we accept that the biblical story of the fall is not pure myth, but has some sort of historical foundation to it, this raises an important question. How does the sinful choice of Adam and Eve go on to affect me? What is it that I inherit from them, and how do I inherit it? Theologians who believe in a historic fall adopt a number of positions on this question, but these divide into two main camps. One group believes that when Adam fell, all humanity at that moment fell with him. It follows from this that we all share in Adam's guilt simply by being human. God looks at us and sees people guilty of Adam's sin. This is known as a 'realist' position, in that it holds that all humanity was really present and implicated in the primal sin of Eden.

The other group believes that we did not fall in Adam at all. Instead, we inherit from Adam some flaw or weakness which results in our becoming guilty of our *own* sin. This stance covers a range of theories, but they can be grouped together as 'non-realist', since they all deny that we share, in a real and immediate way, in the guilt of Adam. Instead, they believe that we somehow inherit the effects of his sin. The issue is whether we are held guilty of Adam's sin, or our own. Do we inherit real guilt, or some type of corruption—a tendency towards sinning? This might sound like a fine distinction, but it raises important issues of biblical theology.

The problem here is that the biblical material is not conclusive either way. Paul writes that 'as in Adam all die, so in Christ all will be made alive' (1 Corinthians 15:22), and that 'sin entered the world through one man' (Romans 5:12). But in neither passage does he explain quite how we all die in Adam, or how through him sin entered the world. Either could be read in terms of us sharing in the real guilt of Adam himself, or else inheriting from him a flawed human nature. We shall briefly outline each of the eight main positions advanced by theologians on this question, and assess their relative strengths and weaknesses. The first three of these assume a 'realist' position; the other five, 'non-realist'.

'Natural'

One of the most ancient understandings of how all people sinned 'in Adam' claims that all of us were actually present in Adam when he sinned. All human nature is bound up in the one man, so his rebellion automatically becomes ours.

How can this be? Advocates of this human-nature or 'natural' position appeal to a particular understanding of the origins of the human soul (which theologians call *traducianism*). This claims that each human being consists of soul and body. When a new child is born, its soul comes into being at the same time as its body, and both are the product of its parents. Like produces like. From this standpoint, it can be argued that a person is 'in the loins' or 'in the body' of his ancestor, an idea found elsewhere in scripture (see Hebrews 7:10). The total make-up of all human beings, spiritual as well as physical, was therefore present 'in Adam', even before they were born. Supporters of the 'natural' view include Augustine and many Lutheran theologians.

Legal

Other Christian thinkers have answered the question using legal categories. We were 'in Adam' because he was our legal representative. The word traditionally used to described the nature of the legal trans-action involved is *imputation*, which literally means 'charging to some-body's account'. In this scenario, God imputes the sin and guilt of Adam instantly to our account. Adam is more than an autonomous individual: he is the legal, divinely appointed head of the whole human race. When the head of humanity sins, his guilt is charged to the account of all of us.

Proponents of this view argue that the most natural reading of Romans 5:12 ('sin entered the world through one man... in this way death came to all men, because all sinned') is that we all sinned at the moment that Adam sinned. Paul's 'all sinned' then becomes not a reference to people's actual sins through history, but their guilty status in Adam. Legal theories based on imputation have found support amongst Reformed (Calvinist) theologians, and were the main theories set out in Puritan writings in the UK and America.

Representation

Other scholars have sought to hold on to a 'realist' view of original sin that sees all humanity as guilty in Adam, but without subscribing to natural or legal explanations. They point out biblical and other difficulties inherent in both these theories (which we shall explore below), but still hold that in some less definable sense Adam had a representative function for all of us.

Such explanations still rely on some idea of the unity of the human race, under the headship of Adam. But this is more likely to be seen in terms of a spiritual unity. When our spiritual representative falls, he pulls us all down with him. An analogy sometimes used to illustrate this position is nationhood. When a head of state declares war on another country, all people in his nation really are at war. And all babies born after this declaration of war are at war too, without their say-so. Maybe our relationship to Adam is something like that of citizens to their head of state. This 'representative' explanation is popular among contemporary evangelical theologians, such as Henri Blocher.

Imitation

Other Christian thinkers reject all 'realist' accounts of original sin. The most extreme form of non-realism is that of Pelagius, whom we met in Chapter 1. Pelagius believed that it was both impossible and morally wrong to hold somebody responsible for something over which they had no control. So he held that there is no real link at all between the sin of Adam and the sin of Adam's descendants. We inherit nothing at all from Adam—neither real guilt, nor a bias towards sinning. According to Pelagius, sin is not a condition at all: there are only sinful actions. We each come into the world as a blank sheet of paper, free to choose good or bad. This is essentially the same as the Jewish and Muslim views of human nature. Each of us is perfectly capable of keeping God's commands.

So how does Pelagius explain the clear fact that people universally make wrong choices? Simply this: that Adam is a bad role model. Adam's sin only directly affected Adam. But we all tend to imitate our parents, in their bad points as well as their good points. So Adam begins a chain of bad example, which is imitated from one generation to the next. What we need is not so much a saviour to save us from the condition of sin as a good example to help us achieve our natural potential. As we have already noted, Pelagianism has resurfaced more recently in the form of 'human potential' and 'self-esteem' psychology, and in theologies influenced by them, as well as 'fringe' Christian groups such as the Unitarians.

Social

Another fairly extreme form of non-realism holds that sin is transmitted through society. On this picture, it is society that is the sinner, more than the individual human being. People are socialized into sin by their participation in a corrupt society. We learn about all sin—gluttony, vice, murder, addictions, vanity, whatever—from the society into which we are born.

Back in the 18th century, the French thinker Rousseau popularized such views. During the 20th century, the 'social gospel' of writers such as Walter Rauschenbusch had a similar emphasis. Rauschenbusch does not deny that there may be something hereditary about evil or damage. He points to various forms of neuroses, disability and even anti-social impulses as something we may inherit genetically. But he explicitly denies the idea of a natural state of sin inherited from Adam. He and other like-minded thinkers put the main blame on society. And those social gospellers who believe in a historic fall (many don't) trace the evils of society ultimately back to Adam. This is the position of many 'liberal' Christians today.

Sexual

Most non-realists, however, find the Pelagian and social accounts of sin inadequate, not least on biblical grounds. They reject the realist stance that we all share in the guilt of Adam, but equally believe that there must be some intrinsic flaw in human nature which may be traced back to Adam—a claim which is, of course, incompatible with theories based merely on bad influence, or the corrupting effects of society.

One way of accounting for this inheritance is in terms of the way life itself is passed on—through sex. On this view, there is something intrinsically fallen in sexual reproduction, particularly the overpowering nature of our sex drive. This loss of control is a penalty of the fall, a sign of the dislocation between mind and body. Before the fall, on this view, sexuality was not associated with such loss of control and raging passion. But now, in the sexual act the soul of the new child is damaged and polluted. Advocates of this view claim that it is impossible to imagine a perfect being conceived in such a way. Sin and sex become inseparable. Only Christ was not conceived sexually, so he alone did not inherit the stain of original sin.

This was the position of some of the early Church Fathers, and it still finds a few supporters today. One of its main protagonists was Augustine, who held the sexual view of transmission alongside the realist, 'natural' view outlined above. It was also the view of Ann Lee, the 18th-century Manchester blacksmith's daughter who led the Christian sect known as the Shaking Quakers, or Shakers, who were particularly influential in 19th-century New England. Lee held that sexual intercourse was the original sin that caused Adam and Eve to fall, and that sex and sin remain inextricably linked. For this reason the Shakers always enforced a strict rule of celibacy among members.

Sickness

Most who favour hereditary transmission nevertheless reject the assumption underlying the last position, that sex is itself sinful. Rather, they have a more positive view of sex, as part of God's good creation, but still hold that original sin is transmitted genetically. As we all descend biologically from Adam, so we inherit in our genes some fatal infection or illness. Sin, like life, is a sexually transmitted disease! Through the centuries, this metaphor of sin as a hereditary sickness has appealed to many thinkers, of all Christian traditions, and many still find it an attractive one. These include Canadian theologian David L. Smith, author of *With Willful Intent* (Bridgepoint, 1994), a major history and theology of the doctrine of sin.

Deprivation

There remains one more account of the transmission of sin in a non-realist framework. It too relies on a basically hereditary understanding, but is suspicious of sexual and medical metaphors. It is the idea that what we inherit from Adam is some sort of deprivation or loss.

At the fall, human nature in Adam forfeited its original righteousness, and God removed from human nature any number of other gifts present before the fall—original grace, a capacity for choosing the right path, divine protection, and so on. The result is an original sin transmitted biologically, from one generation to the next. But what is inherited is not something added to human nature (a virus, lustful passions, or whatever), but something subtracted from our intended humanness.

Adam's loss is our loss—what Adam no longer has, he can no longer hand on to his descendants. The deprivation theory is an attractive one, which has found particular favour among Roman Catholic theologians, as well as thinkers in other church traditions, such as the Puritan Jonathan Edwards, in his 1758 volume *The Great Doctrine of Original Sin Defended*.

Testing the theories

What are we to make of these eight theories about the transmission of original sin? And how can we decide between theories which claim that individuals actually inherit nothing from Adam at all (Imitation and Social theories), those which believe we share in Adam's guilt (Natural, Legal and Representation theories), and those which believe we inherit a flawed nature (Sexual, Sickness and Deprivation theories)? A good place to start might be to eliminate those theories that do not fit the biblical evidence or the evidence of human experience.

First to go must be the Imitation and Social theories, at least in their undiluted form. Each claims, in different ways, that human nature is essentially a blank canvas, that human beings in their natural state are capable of living in relationship with God, and living God's way. But this goes against the plain testimony of the biblical writers, as we discovered in Chapter 3. In the pages of Old and New Testaments alike, we find repeated insistence that 'all have sinned and fall short of the glory of God' (Romans 3:23). And we find the New Testament repeatedly underlining that Jesus Christ died for the sins of the world. What would be the use of an atoning death, if all we needed was a good role model or a more supportive social environment?

The views of Pelagius and the social gospellers alike have to assume that some have managed to reach a state of sinlessness, having shaken off the bad influences of both their forebears and their society. This not only goes against the biblical evidence, it also blatantly contradicts the evidence of real life. Does any of us know anybody who lives in pure, unhindered relationship with God, and never suffers a single moral lapse? Do we live this way ourselves? Could we even imagine living this way? To paraphrase the words of Jesus in John 8:7, 'Let him that is without sin throw the first stone at the doctrine of original sin'! The Pelagian has a sure-fire way of demolishing the doctrine of inherited original sin—by using his free will to live a sinless life. But if he tries this for a month, or even a day, he will see which way the evidence of real life points.

This is not to deny that there may be some truth in both Imitation and Social theories of transmission. It is unquestionably true that our actions are profoundly influenced by parental and social example. But we must conclude that each of these theories on its own fails to do justice to the devastating biblical account of universal human sinfulness.

How about the Natural, Legal and Representation theories, the 'realist' positions that claim we inherit real guilt from Adam? For all their popularity down the centuries, particularly since the Reformation, it has to be said there is surprisingly little biblical support for them—and a good deal against them. We have already noted that the key texts, in Romans 5 and 1 Corinthians, can be taken either way. They each simply make some sort of link between Adam's sin and our own sin and mortality, without specifying the exact nature of that link.

Supporters of our Adamic guilt point to Ephesians 2:3 as crucial support for their position. The verse (in the NIV translation) says, 'We were by nature objects of wrath.' In other words, say Reformed thinkers, our very human nature from birth incurs God's wrathful judgment, irrespective of what actual sins we may have done. On the face of it, the verse does seem to imply that. And this is how many Bible translations render that verse, particularly those from a Reformed stable. However, there is strong reason to question whether the verse actually says this.

Paul, in the original Greek, says this: 'By nature we were children of wrath.' The phrase 'children of' is a typically Hebrew expression for designating character. Paul refers elsewhere to 'children of light' (Ephesians 5:28), where 'children of…' means 'people characterized by…'. Paul nowhere says that the wrath in question is God's. Rather, if the phrase is allowed its usual Hebraic sense, it ought to mean 'wrathful people'. In this case, Paul is simply referring to one expression of our sinful nature—an ill temper.

So where did theologians first get the idea that all people share directly in the guilt of Adam? The answer lies mainly with Augustine, who was working from a bad Latin translation of the New Testament. The Greek of Romans 5:12 includes the words 'because all sinned', a statement about universal human sinfulness. But in Augustine's faulty Latin translation, this was rendered 'in whom all sinned'—leading Augustine to the conclusion that we all share in the sin of Adam, and we all share in his guilt. The problem is, the text does not say this.

Furthermore, there is no biblical evidence for the 'natural' understanding of guilt transference. In fact, it appears to be in tension with other biblical emphases. The 'natural' position relies heavily on a questionable understanding of the human soul. As we saw, it assumes the 'traducian' position, that the soul of a child is somehow derived from the souls of its parents, much as its body comes from their bodies. There is no evidence for this scripturally. And, if the 'natural' position were true, why are we only guilty of this particular sin of Adam? Why should we not be held guilty of all the sins of our parents, even all our ancestors?

How about the legal view, that Adam's sins are imputed to us? Here too there are problems. Even John Murray, a Reformed advocate of imputation, writes: 'When we speak of the sin of Adam as imputed to posterity, it is admitted that nowhere in Scripture is our relation to the trespass of Adam expressly defined in terms of imputation' (*Imputation of Adam's Sin*, Eerdmans, 1959, p. 71). The theory, in other words, has to be read into scripture, rather than out of it.

It also seems to be at odds with the repeated biblical affirmation that individuals are held responsible for their own sins, and not for the sins of their parents (Deuteronomy 24:16; Jeremiah 31:29–30; Ezekiel 18:20), and that the basis for judgment is what we each do—or, more precisely, how our faith is expressed by our deeds (Jeremiah 17:10; Matthew 25:31–46; Romans 2:6; Revelation 2:23). It also seems morally questionable that God should credit the sin of Adam to the account of others, in a purely legal transaction. Fortunately, the Bible does not require any kind of imputation theory to account for how we sinned in Adam.

That leaves the 'non-realist' Sexual, Sickness and Deprivation theories, which each, in different ways, suggest that we inherit from Adam some kind of flawed human nature. All three hold that this flaw then leaves us vulnerable to committing sins of our own, for which we are held personally responsible by God. These positions all have two major advantages over the 'realist' positions.

One is that they affirm the biblical understanding that we are each guilty of our own sins, and not of anybody else's. The other is that they give a plausible, gentler account of how God might treat 'special cases', such as people with learning difficulties and small children. Many have criticized 'realist' accounts of original sin for implying that all are equally guilty before God. What, then, about those who seem unable to choose sin—those with mental illness or learning difficulties, or children too young to make moral choices? On a realist account, these people must be equally guilty before God too. The non-realist alternatives tell a more compassionate story: all people inherit some sort of flawed nature, which is dormant in everybody. People only become guilty when this dormant sin erupts into actual rebellion and wrongdoing.

But how far can we go in supporting the particular non-realist theories we have outlined? Firstly, the Shaker claim that sin is transmitted sexually. This is not simply the claim, common to Sexual, Sickness and Deprivation theories, that the inheritance of sin may have a genetic component. It goes further by claiming that there is something disordered in the sex act itself. Sex is a sign of our fallen nature, and the sex act in procreation is what damages and pollutes the soul of each child who comes into the world.

We can quickly dismiss this theory, which may owe more to the sexual hang-ups of Augustine and subsequent theologians than to the Bible. Indeed, this view can claim no biblical support at all. There is no evidence that sex did not exist before the fall (see Genesis 1:28); the Bible contains an erotic love poem, the Song of Songs; and sexuality is consistently presented as a good gift of God in creation. In Jewish biblical tradition, the ascetic known as a Nazirite (probable lifelong Nazirites named in the Bible are Samuel, Samson and John the Baptist; Paul also took a temporary Nazirite vow) was unique in the ancient world in not having to abstain from marriage or sexual relations.

Likewise, there is no case for the claim sometimes made that Jesus could only be sinless if he was conceived without sexual intercourse. This argument only works if we presuppose that there is something intrinsically disordered and sinful about sex, and that original sin is inextricably linked to the sex act, which scripture nowhere even hints at. Of course, the historic faith has always affirmed both the virginal, non-sexual conception of Christ, and his sinlessness. But we are on shaky ground if we link these two affirmations with a claim that to be truly sinless, Jesus Christ had to be free from any 'taint' of sexuality. That way lies an unhealthy and unbiblical fear of God's good gift of sexual intimacy. And that way lies an unhelpful and unbiblical view of Jesus' mother as one who remained a perpetual virgin—as if this somehow makes her more holy. For all its popularity in Catholic circles, this view has no biblical support and is contradicted by the many references to Jesus' brothers and sisters (for example, Matthew 13:55, 56; Mark 3:31–35). Attempts by some Catholic scholars to explain away these verses as not referring to blood relatives have proved unconvincing.

This leaves the two theories which see the transmission of sin, respectively, as a kind of hereditary illness and as a deprivation of gifts and blessing. These both seem plausible, both biblically and in terms of human experience. The prophet Jeremiah describes the dilemma of the human heart as a sickness (Jeremiah 17:9). We know that certain infirmities can be inherited, and even that forms of addiction and depression might have a genetic component. We also know that a child in the womb and in the early years of infancy will fail to thrive if it is deprived of particular nutrients, protection and love.

We must never forget that such metaphors are only that—metaphors, or analogies to help us make sense of the indescribable. The most we could say is that the transmission of sin might be *something like* passing on a sickness. And we need to remember that the biblical writers nowhere state explicitly how sin is handed on down the generations. But we have found that some of the traditional theories advanced fall outside biblical parameters. It is for each Christian to consider which of the remaining metaphors make best sense, particularly when taken in conjunction with the theory of the identity of Adam they find most convincing (as outlined in the last chapter).

With all this in mind, the analogy some people find helpful today is that of the HIV virus. It is passed on from parent to child. It lies dormant within the human body, but given certain triggers, becomes full-blown AIDS and leads to death. The HIV analogy combines both Sickness and Deprivation metaphors (the virus effectively destroys the body's natural protective mechanisms). It is not so much that we die the death of Adam: rather, we inherit from him a spiritual 'virus' which leaves us weakened and vulnerable, and with a bias towards sin. This tendency towards sin becomes actual sin when people are able to make real spiritual and moral choices. We choose wrongly. We are then held accountable for our sins. Those who, for any reason, never reach a point of moral accountability are not judged for their ignorance.

Some critics will charge that this is still unfair, that nobody should be a victim of a spiritual infection over which they have no control. To these critics, there is a simple response. This is no more unfair than inheriting anything else from our parents, from a tendency towards hay fever to alcoholism. And, as with a tendency towards alcoholism, we still retain moral dignity. We still have some measure of freedom to go with the flow of our damaged nature, or to stand against it and seek help for our condition (even if, as in the case of sin, we are not free to be free from the condition itself). Any accusation of unfairness could only be based on an unreal ideal of individual freedom and autonomy, a claim that we have a right not to be influenced by anything outside ourselves. In reality, we are all profoundly shaped by our genetic inheritance and our environment. If both are polluted by sin, this then becomes a simple fact of life that has to be reckoned with.

There is another way we can look at this whole question of complicity in a state of sin outside our choosing, and that is in terms of the country, region or community we live in. Back in the days of South African apartheid, I met a number of young, white South Africans. Practically all of them expressed abhorrence of the apartheid system, and their opposition to it. Yet the reality was that as white South Africans, they were living off the wealth and advantages of the system they opposed.

This is no criticism of them personally—it is simply to note that whatever our own choices, we inherit some things beyond our control. Similarly, my friends who live in major British ports such as Liverpool or Bristol might look back on the slave trade era with horror. But the fact remains that much of the wealth and infrastructure of their city was built off the proceeds of that trade.

Some things, such as our genetic make-up and the history of the place in which we live, are simply a given. The question then becomes what we do with that given, how we shall now live. What we can't do is go back and rewrite the genes or the history. Our freedom comes up against natural limits.

This idea of sin as an inescapable condition of being human, which we then indulge or resist, could dovetail in with any of the 'falls' in the last chapter. It fits easily with any scenario which sees Adam and Eve as a literal first *Homo sapiens* couple: the whole of human nature is derived from them, including any flaws. It could also fit those scenarios which hold to a more recent Adam and Eve. The only obstacle here is accounting for how the sin of Adam might have been shared by other *Homo sapiens* who, by that stage, had already spread across the globe.

This might be done by combining Sickness and Deprivation theories, with an appeal to the theory of Representation. Without imposing unbiblical categories of others 'naturally' being in Adam, or imputation, we might still suggest that Adam was put in some sort of representative function over all *Homo sapiens* on earth at the time. All theories of the fall, even those which place Eden as recently as 10,000 years ago, agree that Adam is not just any old *Homo sapiens*. He has a unique and distinctive role in the drama of history. His is a unique covenantal relationship with God and other people. As we have said, when a head of state declares war, all people in that nation are in a state of war. When the head of humankind, Adam, sins, all people on earth at that time are caught up in the resulting state of rebellion.

It is not so much that God instantly counts all people guilty of Adam's sin. Rather, it is as if God simultaneously removes a protective hand and divine blessings from the whole species, all over the earth. Why? Because the whole species has made its unilateral declaration of independence, through its appointed representative. As we shall see in the next chapter, this is precisely how Paul defines the 'wrath' of God in his letter to the Romans: a removal of safety fences and divine blessings. The removal of this life-giving fellowship then introduces a failure to thrive, a distortion in human nature, which is then inherited by all subsequent generations. It is as if foetal development is damaged by the withdrawal of life-giving divine grace.

We must not lose sight, however, of the fact that images taken from fields such as genetics are analogies, nothing more. Medical science will never identify a 'sin gene', which medicine or genetic manipulation will one day be able to cure. Sin remains a fundamentally spiritual malaise, invisible but real.

From this base, which draws on images of Deprivation, Sickness and Representation, we can then admit some insights from the more Pelagian positions too. Sin may be inborn, but its effects then spread into the whole culture and are lived out in the real world. Sin becomes something we imitate from our parents (Imitation theory), and we are socialized into by society (Social theory).

But at the end of the day, whatever theories we find most helpful to explain it all, the simple biblical insistence is this: that Adam fell from grace, and we all share in the effects of that fall. If you find all these theories about how this might have happened unhelpful or unnecessary, don't worry! It is the present reality of our condition that really matters. We are fallen.

Did we fall or were we pushed?

In this chapter so far, we have taken for granted that the drama of the transmission of sin involves only human actors. But in earlier chapters we have found clues towards the involvement of something, or somebody, beyond ourselves—a tempter. But mention of the devil tends to evoke howls of protest. The same theologians and sceptics who banished Adam have consigned Satan to the same exile. The devil has been demythologized out of existence in much academic theology and church life alike.

Many theologians refuse to make any kind of identification between the Genesis 3 serpent and the devil, pointing out that there is no explicit mention of the devil in the Old Testament, and that in the few references to a 'Satan', such as in the book of Job, this is hardly the Satan of New Testament and later theology. The Satan of Job is not so much an evil power who opposes God as a member of God's court who has limited powers to test particular individuals. On this account, then, the Genesis serpent is simply a symbol of the option of rejecting God's way. Maybe it is a symbol of the Canaanite fertility cults which were later to rival God for Israel's allegiance. Or maybe the serpent embodies ritual uncleanness under the Jewish Law. According to the categories of 'clean' and 'unclean' animals in Leviticus 11 and Deuteronomy 14, a snake would count as utterly impure.

So can we give a full account of human sinfulness without resorting to the 'mythological' language of the devil and demonology? Should we retain a place for the tempter in Eden, but deny him a role in the transmission of sin? Or should we affirm the place of Satan both in originating and perpetuating human sin? It is to this tricky question that we now turn. We do not have space for a full treatment of the place of the devil in scripture or Christian theology. We shall confine ourselves to two main questions: 'Can we identify the serpent in Genesis as Satan?' and 'Does our answer to this have implications for how sin passes down the generations?'

Serpent, Satan, or both?

First, is this serpent the devil in disguise? This certainly seems to be the claim made at the end of the Bible, in the book of Revelation. In the account of war in heaven, in Revelation 12, we are told, 'The great dragon was hurled down—that ancient serpent called the devil, or Satan, who leads the whole world astray' (12:9). And later in Revelation, an angel from heaven seizes 'the dragon, that ancient serpent, who is the devil, or Satan' (20:2). When the author of Revelation writes 'the devil, or Satan', he is simply translating the same word for different audiences: 'Satan' is the Hebrew for 'accuser', while 'devil' is from the Greek for 'accuser' or 'slanderer'. But in both verses, the reference is unquestionably back to Genesis 3. When Jesus too says that the devil was a liar and a murderer *from the beginning* (John 8:44), again the allusion back to Genesis is clear.

In one breath, Jesus links the fall of Satan with the image of trampling on snakes (Luke 10:18–19), and Paul echoes this same image of Satan being trodden underfoot, as if he were a deadly snake (Romans 16:20). Both are reminiscent of Genesis 3:15, where God's curse on the serpent is that the offspring of woman would crush the serpent's head, as the serpent strikes at the man's heel. There is, then, a New Testament case for identifying the snake-like tempter of Genesis 3 with the devil.

Then what about the biblical assumption that sin and rebellion do not originate with humankind? Jude 6 refers to a fall of heavenly beings: 'And the angels who did not keep their positions of authority but abandoned their own home—these he has kept in darkness, bound with everlasting chains for judgment on the great Day.' And Paul assumes an angelic fall when he says that one who desires leadership 'must not be a recent convert, or he may become conceited and fall under the same judgment as the devil' (1 Timothy 3:6). The New Testament references to Satan falling from heaven and being driven out (Luke 10:18; John 12:31; 16:11; Revelation 12:5–12) may well be figurative allusions to the victory of Christ, in a general sense. But the language of falling could also imply a fall from a former heavenly role. We also noted in the last chapter how the tradition of an angelic fall gives a plausible (perhaps *the* most plausible) account of the origins of sin and brokenness in the natural world.

There is a case, then, for holding to the Christian tradition that the devil is head of the fallen angels, who fell before the fall of humankind. In Genesis 3, the devil appears in the form of a serpent, to spread his own rebellion in Eden. This applies whether we see Eden as the whole, unfallen world, or as the beachhead of a rescue plan in an already fallen world.

Pushing people into sin

But can we take seriously the idea that the devil has some ongoing role in the propagation of sin? Again, this would appear to be the unanimous view of the New Testament writers. Jesus is tempted in the wilderness by the devil (Matthew 4; Luke 4), and repeatedly exorcises demons, all the time alerting his hearers to the reality of the devil. Jesus warns that the devil is poised, ready to snatch the good seed of the word of God from people's hearts (Luke 8:12), and explicitly links the spread of the gospel with the defeat of Satan (Luke 10:18). Paul challenges new believers not to give the devil a foothold (Ephesians 4:27), since the Christian life is bloody warfare against the devil and his schemes, for which we need to wear the armour of God (Ephesians 6:10–18). James urges believers to resist the devil (James 4:7). Peter warns that the devil is prowling around like a roaring lion in search of prey, and needs to be resisted (1 Peter 5:8–9). John even claims that the central and defining reason Jesus Christ came into the world was to destroy the work of the devil (1 John 3:8).

Another biblical clue that the devil plays an ongoing role in pushing people into sin comes in the structure of the book of Revelation. There is strong evidence that the main body of Revelation tells the same story, covering the same period of time, three times over. Chapters 6—19 describe three great judgments of God on the earth. These are portrayed as *seven seals* on documents being opened, *seven trumpets* being sounded, and *seven bowls* of God's wrath being poured out. Each of these three symbolic judgments ends with a description of the Day of the Lord, the final judgment and God's final Kingdom of peace and glory. It appears that we have not so much separate events, arranged chronologically through the book, as the same events looked at from different angles. This is the view of many major commentators on Revelation, including G.R. Beasley-Murray (*Revelation*, Eerdmans/Marshall, Morgan & Scott, 1974), and A.A. Hoekema (*The Bible and the Future*, Eerdmans, 1979).

It is also likely that this period of time is not primarily a description of the end of history, as many readers suppose. Rather, it is a poetic and symbolic portrayal of the whole history of the Church, the ongoing battle between good and evil that is already raging all around us. John, the author of the Apocalypse (as Revelation is also known), has been allowed into the throne room of heaven, and has been allowed to glimpse all human history since Christ from God's standpoint. What he sees is history as a battleground between Christ and Satan. In this light, the events in Revelation 12 are telling us something about the battle for the human heart. They show Satan, desperate to wreak havoc and lure as many people as possible away from Christ, because he knows his time is short (12:12).

It was unquestionably the view of the early Church that Satan was alive and active. The devil is a central concern of the Apostolic Fathers, those early Christian writers said to have known the apostles—including Hermas, Clement of Rome, Ignatius, Polycarp and Papias. Ignatius frequently refers to the devil as 'the ruler of this age'. An exhortation to 'withstand the devil' featured prominently in early catechisms. Rejecting the devil was an important part of baptismal liturgy. The North African theologian Tertullian (160–220) writes, 'When on the point of coming to the water we then... affirm that we renounce the devil and his pomp and his angels.' Around the turn of the second century, the initiation rite into the church in Rome included the statement, 'I renounce you, Satan, and all your service and all your works', and then the bishop signed the candidates with an oil of exorcism (this is the real meaning of the oil still used to make the sign of the cross in baptisms today). The documents of the early Church repeatedly affirm the existence of the devil.

Sin and the devil: some conclusions

It appears, then, that the devil plays a key role in the biblical drama of sin, both in its origins and in its propagation. There is scarcely a writer in the New Testament who does not ascribe a significant role to Satan, and the rejection of the devil was a vital part of the early Church—and remained so down the centuries. Why, then, do so many contemporary Christians struggle with allowing such a place for a real power of evil in their own worldview? Part of the answer must be that Satan comes carrying so much baggage. Medieval images of red demons with horns, toasting forks and goatee beards die hard. Satan has become a figure of fun: witness the movie devils in *The Witches of Eastwick* and *Little Nicky*; TV devils in sketches by the likes of Rowan Atkinson; radio devils as in the BBC's *Old Harry's Game*; cartoon devils by Gary Larson and Scott Adams.

But images of flames, capes and horns owe more to the medieval imagination than to the biblical witness. In scripture, Satan is an enemy less likely to present himself in cape and cloven hoofs than as an angel of light (2 Corinthians 11:14).

Perhaps, in view of our current discussion of the nature of sin, we need to reimagine Satan—not as a glamorous enemy, with a rival kingdom to offer, but as something diseased, something which drains out life (rather like the Dementors in J.K. Rowling's *Harry Potter* stories), a black hole down which goodness is sucked. Even some Christians' talk of a 'personal' devil seems misplaced. God himself is personal—the source of all life and personhood. Human beings made in God's image are also personal, having personal attributes such as creativity, morality and a capacity for relationship. It is hard to see how a fallen spiritual being, which has cut itself off from the source of personhood, could be personal at all. In the Christian worldview, evil has no autonomous existence, no creative power of its own. Evil is an alien intrusion into a good universe, and remains parasitic on goodness.

On this basis, the devil could only be anti-person, a hollow parody of true existence. He (or, perhaps, it) could only wear a mask of personhood, covering the emptiness inside. This would be personhood in its Latin root meaning, where a *persona* was an actor's mask. The devil may appear as an angel, prince, or rival deity, but these are fake *personae*. Perhaps we need to think less in terms of a 'personal' devil who is a centre of spiritual power and can confer power and blessing (this is the mistake of the Satanist) and more in terms of an infection, a computer virus, a leech, or a drain.

Satan's effects can be spread directly into each human heart, as well as through family structures, clubs and gangs, corporate bodies, societies and nations. He seeks to maim the witness of the Church and individual Christians, sowing temptation and seduction, and to keep unbelievers blissfully ignorant of their true state.

Like it or not, the biblical witness about the human condition is that we inherit from Adam a fatal flaw, a bias towards sin which becomes concrete when we are faced with real moral and spiritual choices. At the same time, the choices we believe we are freely making are in fact being subtly influenced from another source outside of ourselves. There is a real force of evil whose sole motive is to pull you and me deeper into sin, and further away from the God in whom alone we can find hope. Human nature is not, as many worldviews, faiths and 'isms' would have us believe, neutral. We are both oriented towards sin, and pushed towards it. We inherit a fatally diseased nature, which leaves us vulnerable to the quack remedies of a sweet-talking, masked deceiver. But these remedies only make our sickness worse.

The Christian claim is not simply that this scenario is to be believed as religious dogma, because the biblical writers or church authorities say so. The claim is that it is true—the truth about the way human nature is. And rival claims which ignore the reality of sin have simply got it wrong, and their solutions could never work, since they are based on a faulty diagnosis of the problem. The Christian claims about sin are offered in the public arena as a truth-claim, a unique and startling insight into what is wrong with the world. Every thinking person is challenged to take this truth-claim seriously and ask whether it fits the evidence of how the world is, and how people are.

If we find the evidence compelling that the sin diagnosis is true, this leaves us in a serious situation. What we need is not just better advice, role models or education, not just enlightenment or more concerted social action. Nor do we just need a bit more will-power. We need something far more radical, something that penetrates to the real heart of the problem—a whole new kind of humanity.

CHAPTER 6

The Rescue Operation

Rock of Ages, cleft for me,
Let me hide myself in thee;
Let the water and the blood,
From thy riven side which flowed,
Be of sin the double cure,
Cleanse me of its guilt and power.
AUGUSTUS TOPLADY (1744–78)

In need of rescue

Where have we reached in our examination of sin? We have found that sin is far from the outdated, irrelevant and judgmental concept that secular sceptics and some Christian critics portray it to be. We found that, on the contrary, the idea of sin offers insights into what is wrong with individuals and society that are more sound than the alternatives. We have claimed that the idea of sin is a credible account of human nature, which is both intellectually satisfying to thinking people and compatible with the best insights of science. We further noted the paradox that a rejection of the sin hypothesis slides into despair and hopelessness, while accepting that the reality of sin offers real hope for transformation.

We found that sin centres on a broken relationship with God, which leads to our being held in the grip of an alien power, participating in a matrix of evil, failing to hit the mark, and then—as our lives disintegrate —we break the moral law. We found that sin is something like a sickness that affects all people, everywhere, and leads to death. And we found that it has its origins first in an angelic fall in the heavenly realms, and is transmitted via Adam, the representative head of humanity. On biblical grounds, we rejected the idea that all people are automatically held guilty of the sin of Adam, finding more evidence that we each inherit from Adam a bias towards sin, which becomes concrete the moment we are faced with real moral decisions. We saw, too, how we are at the same time oriented towards sin, and pushed towards it.

This background helps to make sense of the biblical claim that human nature, left to its own devices, is fatally flawed. This insight runs counter to the naïve humanism which claims that human nature is fundamentally good, and that a utopian society may be attainable through human effort alone. Here it is the Christian, and not the humanist, who demonstrably has the evidence of history on her side. This leads, in turn, to the biblical insistence that we need a rescuer, saviour, or redeemer. In the pages of the Bible this saviour is identified as Jesus of Nazareth, about whom some extraordinary claims are made. But exactly how does Jesus function as the one who saves the world from sin? We shall explore this shortly. First, we need to look briefly at two proposals concerning the role of Jesus that have been suggested, each of which contains some positive insights but ultimately falls short of the biblical witness.

The good example theory

A popular explanation of how Jesus Christ is our saviour centres on the idea that he offers us a good example to follow. This is an idea that can claim some biblical support. We are to love God 'as Christ loved us' (Ephesians 5:2). We are to follow Jesus' example of longsuffering (1 Peter 2:19–22), and his humility and obedience (Philippians 2:5–8). The 'Jesus as good example' theory takes different forms.

Jesus as moral example

In the fifth century, Pelagius put forward the view that God's answer to human weakness is the good moral example of Jesus Christ. This view was resurrected in the 19th century by German theologians Adolf von Harnack (1851–1930) and Albrecht Ritschl (1822–89), and many others in our own day. In this scenario, the 'real' Jesus was essentially a moral teacher and role model, possibly the greatest teacher of ethics who ever lived. Our role is to live by his moral standards, thereby creating generous and loving communities. This is our 'salvation'.

Jesus as spiritual example

Many mystical religious traditions see Jesus as a role model of spirituality or God-consciousness. For most New Agers, Jesus is a spiritual guide or master, one who experienced a 'higher consciousness'. For many Hindus, Jesus is one spiritual guide among many, or even one god among many. Some thinkers within the Christian tradition have used the language of transformed awareness too. For Friedrich Schleiermacher (1768–1834), Jesus is the 'mediator of God-consciousness'. For Matthew Fox, the historical Jesus is just one incarnation of a 'Cosmic Christ'. He is an archetypal figure who helps us all to realize our own essential divinity. For Jack Spong, Jesus is one who embodies divine love, and was vibrantly alive. Jesus, in turn, can inspire all of us to love, and to be truly ourselves.

Jesus as ideological example

Others have found in Jesus the pioneer of their own hopes of political and social liberation. For liberation theologians, Jesus is a revolutionary, the herald of a new egalitarian social order. For many Christian socialists, Jesus is a pioneer socialist; for conservatives he is an arch-conservative. For social-gospellers such as Walter Rauschenbusch (1861–1918), Jesus is a preacher of social reform. For some feminists, Jesus is the great challenger of patriarchy. For some gays, Jesus is the one who affirms their struggle. For some environmentalists, Jesus is the one who reveals the possibilities for humans living in harmony with the planet.

All three varieties of the 'good example' theory have one thing in common. They believe in a Jesus who exemplifies human potential, a trailblazer who helps us tap into our own inner resources for the good of ourselves and society. They are all *subjective* approaches to the role of Jesus. We each look at Jesus and see in him a vision of what we can each become—morally, spiritually, politically. There is at least a grain of truth in all of these. As we noted, New Testament writers do invite their readers to follow the example of Jesus Christ. The Jesus of the scriptures clearly does have an extraordinary level of God-consciousness. And there is a clear emphasis on liberation in the teachings of Jesus.

But as well as their grain of truth, all these 'good example' theories contain two serious flaws. The first is that theirs is essentially a humanist agenda, covered with a light religious veneer. The whole movement is 'bottom-up', starting from the individual's right to define the terms of the faith for herself, rather than 'top-down' in submitting to a higher authority. Jesus becomes merely a teacher of human potential. He is a mirror in which people see their own reflection looking back at them. The idea that God in Christ might be fundamentally subverting all human-potential agendas is quietly ignored. The possibility that human moral achievement, spiritual progress and political change might be at best secondary issues, and at worst a waste of time, are never countenanced. These are theories that take a personal agenda and project it on to Jesus, with little interest in whether Jesus himself might have had a very different agenda.

There is always the danger that such ideology-driven approaches to Jesus will harm even the grain of truth their advocates draw from the New Testament. It is true that Jesus advanced an ethic of love, but can we really assume that our definitions of love are ones that Jesus would recognize? It is true that Jesus had a unique consciousness of God, but this is of the personal Father-Creator of the Hebrew scriptures—not the impersonal, pantheistic forces of New Age and Eastern religions, or some unbiblical notion of our own inner 'divinity'. And it is true that the gospel of Jesus is liberating, but who are we to define what kind of liberation we most need? If we define the terms of our own liberation, and see Jesus as chief revolutionary, we may well find ourselves craving to be 'liberated' into what the biblical writers would see as a deeper state of sin or enslavement. In fact, if it is true that we are each oriented towards sin, and pushed towards it, such self-deception becomes a virtual certainty.

The second flaw in these instances of the 'good example' theory is that they fail to do justice to the biblical material on how Jesus saves. Here, the evidence points decisively away from a purely subjective interpretation. The language of the New Testament indicates that with Jesus, something objective has really happened that profoundly affects human nature, the whole created order, even God himself. Whether you and I choose to participate in it or not, something real is going on out there. The Kingdom of God has come near, a victory has been won, an antidote to the sickness of sin has been made available, the matrix of sin has been dealt a death blow, a whole new kind of humanity is made real. This is not the subjective language of good example or released potential. This is something objective and radical.

The hostile God theory

The 'good example' theory is particularly prevalent among Christian social activists. A second theory can typically be heard in some popular evangelical preaching. It is the idea that the natural attitude of God towards human beings and the whole creation is one of hostility. The Father burns with anger at our sin, and demands that this sin be punished. However, when Jesus takes our punishment on the cross, God's anger is turned away. His attitude changes from hostility to love.

Superficially, this theory sounds biblical. In fact, it is sometimes expounded as *the* biblical teaching on salvation—often with great passion. Jonathan Edwards' 'Sinners in the Hands of an Angry God', which we met in Chapter 1, presupposes something like this theory. In its favour, the theory does take deadly seriously the reality of sin, unlike the theories of many liberal theologians. This view does come close to some of the biblical teaching on salvation, close enough to be confused with what the biblical writers actually say. But as it stands, we have to reject this too as an inadequate theory. The main reason is that it gives an unbiblical picture of God.

It is simply not true to say that God's attitude to his creation, especially the human creation, is one of hostility. Those sections of the Bible most loved and quoted by many Christians, John 3:16 and Romans 5:8, both underline this forcefully. John 3:16 tells us that God sent his only Son into the world to save it—not because he was hostile to it, but because 'he so *loved* the world'. And Paul in Romans tells us that 'God demonstrates *his own love* for us in this: while we were still sinners, Christ died for us' (Romans 5:8).

It is true that Paul also writes in Romans of the wrath of God against sin (for example, 1:18; 5:9). What this cannot possibly mean, though, is that in our natural, sinful condition God hates and rejects us, but that once Jesus has absorbed our punishment, God loves us. Two observations about this wrath of God must be made. First, the only appropriate biblical framework for understanding God's wrath has to be a family one. A loving father remains committed to his wayward son, even as he hates, say, the addiction that has taken a grip of him. The wrath is not opposed to the love: it is a direct consequence of it. Real love cannot abide anything that destroys or alienates the loved one— which, of course, is precisely what sin does.

Secondly, God's wrath is neither cold vindictiveness or active hostility, as some preachers have presented it. Paul describes, in Romans 1, how God's wrath against sin actually operates: God allows people to keep on going down the path they have chosen. This might not sound very wrathful to people raised in a culture like ours, which prizes personal freedom of choice above all else. But remember that in a biblical worldview, what matters is not the choosing, but choosing wisely. The parties involved here are sinful humanity and a loving God. When sinful people choose to go their own way, they invariably choose a path of disintegration and death. God's wrath is seen in the removal of his protective hand. The safety fences are down, and God allows people to pursue their own desires and lusts (Romans 1:18–32). The Father says to the rebellious child, 'OK, have it your way,' even while he longs for family reconciliation, and for his child to be free from whatever is messing him up.

This is both Paul's understanding of how God's wrath operates and the vision of divine wrath offered in the Old Testament too. Paul's phrase 'God gave them over...' (Romans 1:24) actually echoes God's own verdict on centuries of dealings with his chosen people, Israel: 'But my people would not listen to me; Israel would not submit to me. *So I gave them over* to their stubborn hearts to follow their own devices' (Psalm 81:11–12, emphasis mine).

Despite references to God's wrath, then, it is not the case that the death of Jesus has somehow changed God's attitude to us. No biblical verse suggests that God's basic attitude to us has been changed by Jesus, from anger to love. The biblical witness is unmistakable: God loves us, full stop.

This places a question mark over some popular diagrams for explaining salvation, such as the one showing ourselves and God as two steep cliffs with an impassible gulf in between. The cross of Christ is then drawn as a bridge across the gulf, showing how the two parties can be reconciled. This implies a picture of God as stony-faced and aloof from sinful humanity. But biblically, nothing could be further from the truth.

Even images from popular devotion such as the lost and rescued sheep raise more questions about God than they answer. In its traditional form, this image pictures the sinner as a sheep who has fallen over a precipice, and is caught fast in a thicket. Jesus, the shepherd, leans over and pulls the sheep to safety. But where is God the Father in this scenario? He is less a divine presence than a divine absence. How can we enter a family relationship with an absence? Despite the fact that many Christians down the years have found such analogies helpful, real questions have to be asked about whether they do justice to the biblical portrait of God.

Tom Smail writes of the danger of 'encouraging people to hide behind the coat tails of a loving Jesus to shield them from the anger of a vengeful God' (*Once and For All*, DLT, 1998, p. 86). This is uncomfortably close to the way many well-meaning Christians present the message of salvation. And it is uncomfortably close to many people's actual experience of spirituality. This is not only true in evangelical circles. It also appears in popular Catholic devotion, where Mary is sometimes presented alongside her son as gentler and more approachable than God. In both evangelical and Catholic forms, such a spirituality is actually deeply unChristian. God the Father becomes at best a judge and lawgiver, at worst an unapproachable and vindictive despot—hardly the 'Abba' of the Lord's Prayer, or the loving father in Jesus' parable of the prodigal son.

Some will respond that this image of God as angry and vengeful is drawn from the Old Testament. People often say that the God of the Old Testament is a God of anger and judgment, but the God of the New Testament is a loving Father. This is not only wrong, it is disastrous in its effects. It leads many people to write off the whole Old Testament as a saga of legalism and barbarity, and confirms them in their view that God is 'really' remote and vindictive. Quite how wrong this view is becomes clear from reading the writings of the prophet Hosea, from around 800 years before the birth of Christ, which offer the clearest Old Testament window into the character and motives of God.

Hosea shows that the two words that best sum up God are 'lover' and 'father'. God is a passionate lover, who remains faithfully besotted despite the infidelities of his beloved (Hosea 1—6). And God is a compassionate father, taking the tiny child he loves by the hand and teaching him to walk (Hosea 11). The message of Hosea is that if God shows anger, this anger is the pain of an abandoned lover, whose wife has become a serial adulteress. It is the grief of a neglected father.

God's anger in the Old Testament era is directed against the fertility cults of Israel's neighbours, which were leading God's people into spiritual adultery and moral chaos. Such accounts can be found in Deuteronomy 7 (the command to destroy nations worshipping Baal, Ashtoreth and Molech), and Numbers 25 (the killing of the Israelite men who had sex with Moabite women and worshipped Moabite gods). And God's anger is directed against those nations and his own people who trample on justice (among many passages, see Amos 8 and Isaiah 58). In other words, God cares above all else about relationships: divine–human relationships and human–human relationships. And he won't for ever stand idly by when infidelity, abuse and injustice are rife.

God's anger is motivated by his compassion. He gives these other nations, and his own people, many opportunities to repent. When he judges them, it is as a last desperate resort. From God's perspective, the stakes are high. Temple prostitution, child sacrifice, injustice and oppression, the occult—unless God puts a stop to such activities, the surrounding nations, God's own people, maybe the whole of humanity, will be lured past the point of no return.

Again we need to remember that in a biblical worldview what matters is not freedom of choice, but choosing wisely. We can only make sense of God's Old Testament acts of judgment when we view them through biblical assumptions: God is a passionate lover and a compassionate father; humanity only has meaning and fulfilment in relationship with God; rejection of God is the ultimate tragedy; when God acts in judgment this is an act of mercy, holding people back from the devastating consequences of their wrong choices.

Any theory which presupposes a God who is remote, hostile or judgmental falls far short of this biblical portrait.

A familiar dilemma

So if salvation is more than copying Jesus' good example, and we are wide of the mark if we claim that Jesus changes God's mind from hostility to love, then is there a better way to understand the Christian idea of salvation? Here we come across a familiar dilemma.

Back in Chapter 5, we found a clear insistence in the Bible that sin is linked in some profound and essential way with Adam. Less immediately obvious is precisely how Adam's sin is linked to ours. We had to follow a trail of scattered clues in order to piece together a coherent picture. Even then, we had to remind ourselves that any metaphors we use are just that—metaphors. They are ways of helping our limited minds to grasp something profound and cosmic in scope, which touches on the deepest mysteries of human nature and God's dealings with the world. The best we can hope for is analogies that ring true, both to the language of the Bible and human experience.

Something similar applies to salvation. The New Testament writers nowhere set out a tidy and systematic doctrine of salvation. What they do is to proclaim that Jesus Christ is the answer to human sin, and use a wide range of different images to help us to grasp how this might work. Here, too, we need to remind ourselves that no single image exhausts all possibilities, and that even our best metaphors are just metaphors, helpful but not exhaustive. The reality of salvation remains a profound mystery, a relationship to be entered, even while our minds are still grasping for a picture-language to do it justice.

Identification

But is there a key that unlocks more doors than others, and helps to set us on the right path? Is there a central or controlling image in the New Testament that helps us understand the mystery of God's rescue plan? I believe there is—and the key word is *identification*. True, the word itself is not used regularly in the Bible. But what this word represents is everywhere assumed, and it gives a helpful framework in which we can make sense of the range of metaphors the Bible writers do use.

Why 'identification'? Historic Christianity has always held that Jesus Christ is both human and divine. The legends of the ancient world may have featured heroes, such as Hercules, whose parentage was said to be both divine and human. But the extraordinary claim of the Christian faith is that in Christ the dreams of the ancient storytellers have become reality. Jesus of Nazareth is the only person who has ever lived who really does combine both a fully human and a fully divine nature. Because of this, Jesus is able to identify fully with both us and God. Uniquely, he knows from the inside what it is to be both God and man.

For the moment, we need to note in particular that the New Testament writers are at pains to stress how Jesus Christ identifies with humanity. At his incarnation, he takes on human flesh and lives among us (John 1:14). At his birth he is called Immanuel, 'God with us' (Matthew 1:23). At his baptism he stands in solidarity with sinners needing to repent and be cleansed (Luke 3:21–22). He is tempted in every way, as we are (Luke 4:1–13; Hebrews 4:15). He eats, sleeps, loves, laughs, weeps, feels anger, and even knows what it is to feel abandoned by God (Mark 15:34). He lives a human life and dies a messy and painful human death.

Identification and salvation

So how does the identification of Jesus with both us and God help us with our problem of sin? To grasp this, we must focus on his identification with humanity in all its sinfulness. The most striking claim made about this can be found in 2 Corinthians 5:21: 'God made him who had no sin *to be sin* for us' (my emphasis).

In other words, Jesus identifies so intimately with our fallen humanity that he even identifies with our sin—even though he himself is without sin. He takes on to himself the full, destructive effects of human sin— the broken relationships, the falling short, the lawbreaking, and so on. God's way of dealing with sin is to put it to death. Jesus so identifies with our sin that he pulls it down to the grave with him. And as we identify with Christ, we also identify with his rising from the dead. His new life becomes ours, too. In each case, he does for us what we could never do for ourselves.

This helps to explain the language of sacrifice applied in the Bible to the death of Jesus. In Old Testament sacrifice, the person bringing an animal or bird for sacrifice becomes identified with that creature. The death of the animal replaces the death of the sinful person. At the same time, the life of the animal which is offered up to its creator is identified with the offering up of the life of the person, as an obedient 'living sacrifice'.

Jesus identifies with humanity not only in his death and resurrection, but in his life too. Here, at last, is a man who is fully obedient to God (Mark 14:36; Hebrews 5:8–9). The whole biblical drama has been a story of God entering into covenant relationship with human beings, but that covenant being repeatedly broken on the human side: in Eden, in the life of Israel, and on through history. But here at last is a new kind of humanity, who keeps the human side of the covenant with God, a humanity in right relationship to God, because Christ also shares the nature of God himself. Jesus is the fulfilment of the covenant, the one able to offer to God the 'yes' he longs to hear from humanity, because Jesus alone is untainted by sin.

This helps us make sense of Paul's important Adam–Christ parallels (Romans 5; 1 Corinthians 15). In both passages, Paul draws up a contrast between Adam as the representative head of the old, sinful humanity, and Jesus Christ as the head of a new humanity. The 'old' humanity is identified with Adam, the 'new' humanity in solidarity with Christ. There are now two different ways to be human. Paul's letters are full of strong imagery of identification with Christ, in his life, death and resurrection: 'I have been crucified with Christ and I no longer live, but Christ lives in me. The life I live in the body, I live by faith in the Son of God, who loved me and gave himself for me' (Galatians 2:20).

Neither is this theme of identification only present in the writings of Paul. The anonymous writer of the letter to the Hebrews makes it clear that identification is at the heart of his understanding of salvation. And he explicitly links this identification to Christ's victory over sin and the forces of evil: 'Since the children have flesh and blood, he too shared in their humanity so that by his death he might destroy him who holds the power of death—that is, the devil... For this reason he had to be made like his brothers in every way' (Hebrews 2:14–17).

Some Christian thinkers have used other words than identification to describe our solidarity with Christ. How do these other words measure up to the biblical witness? Some talk of 'substitution'. In a real sense, Jesus Christ is our substitute, in that he died our death and took on to himself the burden of our sin. But substitution language can only coherently apply to the death of Christ. It is less appropriate for handling the biblical idea that we can now be joined to Christ and participate in his risen life. That part is not so much substitution as fellowship, or incorporation. People whose model of salvation is based on substitution will inevitably look backwards and emphasize crucifixion as the heart of the gospel. This is a vital emphasis, but it is only part of the biblical account of salvation—which is also about being joined to Christ in his life and resurrection too.

Other Christians have claimed that Christ is our 'representative'. This is helpful as far as it goes, but is rather weak language. Most representatives do what we ask them to, and we remain more or less in control. But in the case of Christ, he takes on himself the whole of the human condition, puts sinful humanity to death and opens the way to a whole new human nature. It is not so much that he represents us, as that we are grafted into what he has achieved. The language of identification is closer to the facts of the matter, or perhaps a similar term such as 'solidarity' or 'union'. Paul writes of believers' union with Christ in his death and resurrection (Romans 6:5), and of our encouragement at being united with Christ (Philippians 2:1), even while we each retain our own distinct identity. Paradoxically, it is only as we are united with

Christ that we begin to find our true selves and discover who we were meant to be.

Becoming identified

So how do we participate in this new humanity? Paul talks of believers being 'in Christ' (a healthy corrective to the self-centred emphasis in some churches on 'Jesus in me'). But how do we get to be 'in Christ'? Here, the parallel with Adam diverges. All people, everywhere, share in Adam's sin, simply by being human. But identification with Christ is a 'narrow path', which only a few find (Matthew 7:13–14). We remain identified with Adam until we respond to God's invitation to be identified with Jesus. And in the New Testament, there are two parts to this response: heartfelt, committed faith in Christ, and baptism.

On the day of Pentecost 3,000 people followed Peter's instruction to repent and be baptized (Acts 2:38). In the New Testament, an un-baptized Christian is a contradiction in terms. Jesus' 'great commission' to his disciples before he left them was, 'Go therefore and make disciples of all nations, baptizing them in the name of the Father and of the Son and of the Holy Spirit' (Matthew 28:19). Biblically, it seems that baptism is not simply a sign of becoming a Christian, or public witness to conversion. It is actually part of the process: 'Don't you know that all of us who were baptized into Christ Jesus were baptized into his death? We were therefore buried with him through baptism' (Romans 6:3–4); 'This water symbolizes baptism that now saves you' (1 Peter 3:21). Baptism brings us into the Church, Christ's 'body' (1 Corinthians 12:13).

How does baptism do this? Again, we need to use language of identification. The power of baptism is as a gateway to identification with Christ. The water of baptism is a picture-language loaded with wider meanings, particularly overtones of death. It is an image of washing (purification, old self washed away), drowning (death to an old self), the flood (judgment, death and rescue), and crossing the Red Sea (death and liberation). At the same time, the waters of baptism are the waters of new life: waters of the womb, water that sustains life. As we go under the water of baptism we are baptized into the death of Jesus Christ. As we rise from the water, we rise to a new kind of life.

So the Bible stongly implies that the sacrament of baptism actually 'does' something for us. In theological jargon, baptism is 'instrumental': it incorporates us into Christ. Does it then follow that anybody who has been baptized is automatically a Christian—that if you are baptized, there is no need for deepening personal commitment, church fellowship, and so on? Far from it.

Being a Christian is a coin with two sides. One side is baptism, but the other is faith. This faith involves repentance, a turning away from sin, and a turning to the wonder of Jesus Christ. And in order to be able to repent and have faith in Christ, people need to have heard about him. This explains Paul's urgency in calling believers to mission and proclamation: 'How can they believe in the one of whom they have not heard? And how can they hear without someone preaching to them?' (Romans 10:14). The issue with faith is not whether a person came to faith suddenly as an adult, or has grown in faith slowly over the years. Neither is 'better' or 'more biblical' than the other. The real issue is whether that person now has a living faith that unites them to Jesus Christ, a union sealed in baptism.

Baptism and faith: both sides are needed. We can put this another way. Baptism is like the church service in which my wife and I were married many years ago, and the certificate we received to confirm our marriage was officially recognized. Together, these were our legal gate of entry into marriage. But the *inner reality* which makes our marriage is the love and commitment between the two of us. Both parts are needed for our marriage to be real. We need to be able to look back on our wedding day, and look at our wedding certificate. But we also need to live out the reality of being married day by day, and not live apart or in a state of permanent warfare. Otherwise, the wedding day and certificate count for very little!

So if I come to faith, is this faith alone enough to make me a Christian? Biblically speaking, I should be baptized for my conversion to be complete. And if I have been baptized, is that enough to make me a Christian? No! I need to live out the reality of which baptism was the entry and sacrament. And that reality is a life of passionate, committed faith.

Infant baptism?

A brief digression is in order here. Many Christians argue, persuasively, that in the New Testament baptism only happens after a person has come to faith in Christ. It is therefore for those who have made a conscious choice, not infants—who may or may not come to a living faith over time. But historically, most churches have baptized infants—including my own church, the Church of England. Why?

We have three main reasons. Firstly, children were part of the Old Testament 'church'. God's covenant with Israel was not limited to adults. Male infants received the physical mark of the covenant, circumcision, long before they could respond personally to God. By extension, children brought up in Christian homes, under the New Covenant, should be able to receive the mark of the new covenant. Only now, the mark is available to male and female alike. Secondly, when non-Jews converted to Judaism, the whole family was baptized. Convert baptism wasn't reserved for adults who knew what they were doing. It was for the whole household. Ancient Israel had a high view of family solidarity, unlike our individualistic society. And thirdly, we know that whole families were baptized in the New Testament, such as those of the Philippian jailer (Acts 16:15) and Cornelius (Acts 11:14). It is hard to imagine that such family baptisms didn't include young children.

But this raises an apparent difficulty. It means that for many people, who were baptized as infants, the two sides of the Christian 'coin'— baptism and living faith—might actually be years apart. Does this matter? Apparently not. The answer is simply to make sure you have both.

So if you were baptized as a baby, but come to a living faith later in life, should you be rebaptized? Absolutely not. Baptism is unrepeatable. A couple with a lacklustre marriage, whose relationship then dramatically improves and whose love comes alive like never before, do not need to remarry. Similarly, your first baptism was entirely valid—be happy that you are at last entering into its full meaning. A rite of 'reaffirmation of baptismal vows', available in most churches, might be helpful—just as some couples find it meaningful to reaffirm their marriage vows.

Staying identified

If we become identified with Christ through faith and baptism, how do we stay identified? Again, the answer is through faith and sacrament. There are two sacraments of the gospel commanded by Jesus in the New Testament. One is baptism, the other holy communion, or eucharist (from a Greek word meaning 'to give thanks'). If baptism is the sacrament of initiation, eucharist is the sacrament of continuation.

In the Catholic, Orthodox and Lutheran traditions, followers of Jesus believe that they eat and drink the body and blood of Christ in a very real way at the eucharist. In Reformed, Evangelical and Pentecostal traditions, the eucharist is also a moment of intense communion with Christ—not so much because the bread and wine themselves become charged up with his presence, but because Christ comes to us by his Spirit as we receive the elements. Either way, eucharist is about identification with Jesus Christ. It is a moment when our identification with him is both proclaimed and made real.

But again, this only happens in the context of living faith. The Christian life is a life of faith and trust in God, and this faith also needs to be expressed in a range of ways, such as prayer, study of the Bible, worship, and fellowship with other believers. The main reason these are vital for the life of faith is that in each of these areas a very real identification with Christ is going on.

In his letter to the Romans, Paul tells them that prayer is actually a participation in the life of God. I, as a believer, have the Holy Spirit of Christ living in me. The Spirit joins me to Christ (this is Paul's argument in Romans 8). So prayer is not simply something I 'do'. It is allowing the Spirit of Christ to communicate through me to the Father, calling him *Abba*, just as Jesus did (Romans 8:15). Prayer is an activity within the life of God but, as people united with Christ, we have the privilege of being a channel through which this happens. Likewise, in Bible study we stand, awestruck, in the place of those who first met Jesus Christ. Worship is our total self-offering to Christ and our rededication to a life of service. And in fellowship with other believers we participate in the 'body of Christ' on earth, an image we shall explore below.

Nailing sin

The heart of salvation, then, is being identified with Jesus Christ, in his life, death and resurrection. We are now in a position to explore the various metaphors the New Testament writers use to describe this salvation, and see how they specifically answer each of the dimensions of sin outlined in Chapter 3. In that chapter we saw how sin is simultaneously a broken relationship with God, an alien power, a matrix of evil, failing to hit the mark, and lawbreaking. We shall take one at a time and see how God's rescue operation, in which we become identified with Christ, nails each one.

A broken relationship

We have seen how the essence of sin lies in a broken relationship with God. However, for believers identified with Christ, this broken relationship is replaced with an intimate relationship. We share in the sonship of Jesus. This relationship is expressed biblically in three potent family metaphors: regeneration, reconciliation and adoption.

Regeneration

We find significant language of new birth in the teaching of Jesus (John 3:3–8), and John (for example, 1 John 5:1). In some circles today, phrases such as 'born again' have assumed an almost political function —denoting a certain type of Christian, or as a way of writing off a particular type of religious experience. But the theme of regeneration is an important one in biblical faith. The experience of being united with Christ is nothing less than that of dying to an old self, and being reborn as a new person. New birth is, of course, an image taken from a family context. We share in Christ's death, and are reborn with him to a new life in God's family.

Reconciliation

Another relational image used by Paul to highlight the restoration of relationship with God is reconciliation. He writes, 'Once you were alienated from God... But now he has reconciled you by Christ's physical body' (Colossians 1:21–22), and that 'when we were God's enemies, we were reconciled to him through the death of his son' (Romans 5:10). In 2 Corinthians 5, Paul further outlines his theme of reconciliation, adding that God has committed to believers this message of reconciliation, and urging all his readers to be reconciled to God through Christ.

Adoption

Perhaps the clearest way Paul expresses the restoration of relationship between us and God is with his image of adoption into God's family. He tells the Roman Christians, 'For you did not receive a spirit that makes you a slave again to fear, but you received the Spirit of sonship. And by him we cry, "*Abba*, Father"' (Romans 8:15). The word Paul uses for sonship is the Greek word *huiothesia*, 'adoption'. Paul uses the same word when he tells the Galatians that God sent his Son so that those redeemed 'might receive the full rights of sons' (Galatians 4:5–6). Again, Paul's theme is adoption. Our identification with Jesus Christ is highlighted by Paul's use of the Aramaic term *Abba*, a family word for Father. God's Spirit inside us calls out to God using the very language of Jesus himself.

At the heart of the biblical language of slavery and sonship lies a profound and ironic parallel. The Son becomes a slave so that slaves can become sons. Jesus Christ, despite his divine nature, took on the attitude of a servant (Philippians 2:6–7), even adopting the posture of the Roman slave by washing his disciples' feet (John 13:1–17). He did this so that we, slaves to the alien power of sin, might become adopted members of God's family: 'You are no longer a slave, but a son; and since you are a son, God has made you also an heir' (Galatians 4:7).

Regeneration, reconciliation, adoption: all images of restored relationship into the Father's family. Here, then, is the heart of the matter. Sin breaks relationship. Salvation restores what was broken.

A woman I know called Kathy came to faith relatively late in life, never having attended a church or read the Bible. She described her experience of conversion to me as being like coming home for the first time. She felt like a child being wrapped up in a big, family blanket by a loving parent. At that point, she did not even know that there were such things as biblical metaphors of salvation. But her own experience told her what was going on: it was a homecoming, an adoption into the Father's family.

An alien power

If sin is also a hostile power, salvation is about liberation, redemption and ransom from the grip of this power. It is also about liberation from the power of the evil one.

Liberation

In the biblical story, the Exodus of the people of Israel out of Egypt is a defining moment. God is revealed as a God who liberates captives. When Jesus begins his ministry in Galilee, he chooses as his statement of purpose some verses from the prophet Isaiah, claiming that the Spirit of God is upon him to 'proclaim freedom for the prisoners' and 'to release the oppressed' (Luke 4:18). It is clear from Jesus' subsequent ministry that the liberation he has in mind is no mere political liberation from the Roman occupying forces. He tells Jewish leaders that everyone who sins is a slave to sin, but that 'if the Son sets you free, you will be free indeed' (John 8:34–36). In his coming, people are liberated from the forces of evil (for example, Luke 4:31–37). In his life, he resists the wiles of the evil one (Matthew 4:1–11), and through his death and resurrection, he frees people from the devil's power (Hebrews 2:14–15).

Paul echoes the same theme of liberation: 'Where the Spirit of the Lord is, there is freedom' (2 Corinthians 3:17); 'It is for freedom that Christ has set us free. Stand firm, then, and do not let yourselves be burdened again by a yoke of slavery' (Galatians 5:1). He even talks of the whole created order sharing in this liberation from bondage (Romans 8:21). Salvation is massive in its scope, rippling out beyond the human world to a vision of the whole cosmos liberated.

How is this liberation linked to what we have said about the believer's identification with Christ? Simply this: the old humanity was a slave to sin. That humanity was put to death for those who are in Christ. The slave nature has died, leaving a new humanity, liberated from the alienation and power of sin.

Redemption and ransom

Related images are of redemption and ransom. Both are images of recovering or releasing something, at a price. In ancient Roman society it was a common practice for slaves to be bought out of their slavery. So deliverance from the slavery of sin would quite naturally spring to Paul's mind as an image of salvation. He writes of Christ 'giving himself as a ransom' for all people (1 Timothy 2:6). But images of ransom and redemption are not limited to Paul.

Zechariah prophesies over the infant Jesus, praising God because in this child God 'has come and has redeemed his people' (Luke 1:68). And Peter tells his readers, 'For you know that it was not with perishable things such as silver or gold that you were redeemed... but with the precious blood of Christ' (1 Peter 1:18–19). It is pushing the metaphor too far to speculate on who 'receives' this ransom payment. The image simply underlines the profound truth that to achieve liberation, a costly ransom price must be paid.

A few weeks ago I was shopping in London's Tottenham Court Road, when I heard a whimpering noise. I looked down and saw a dog, cowering beside a man who was begging at the side of the road. Every time the dog whimpered, the man would punch or kick it, and the poor dog bore the scars of years of maltreatment. Many shoppers were horrified and averted their eyes, or crossed the road to avoid the ugly scene.

Eventually, one passer-by was so sickened by what was happening to the dog that he opened his wallet, waved a banknote in front of the beggar and offered to buy the dog from him. The man said he would take the dog home, show it love, and treat it as a treasured family pet. He was acting as a redeemer, paying the price to secure freedom from tyranny. The dog was being ransomed, by a new and loving master who would not abuse it, but instead give it all the privileges of family membership.

In this story, images of ransom, liberation and adoption belong together. Far from being conflicting or mixed metaphors, each reinforces the others. The same would have been true of these same three images in Paul's day. As Mark Stibbe points out in his helpful book *From Orphans to Heirs* (BRF, 1999) when Paul uses the image of adoption, he has in mind adoption under Roman law (there was no Jewish rite of adoption at the time). A frequent pattern of Roman adoption was that a couple who were full Roman citizens would find a slave couple, and offer to pay money for the right to bring up one of their sons as their own. This might sound heartless to us, but the slave couple would often agree to such a transaction. After all, their son, through this adoption, would become a free man and the legal heir to the master's whole estate.

This is the arrangement Paul almost certainly has in mind as he slips between images of adoption, ransom and liberation. One process of adoption that he, as a Roman citizen, would have known involved a 'ransom' payment, and a transfer from slavery to freedom. As such, it makes an ideal image of salvation. We gain *liberty* from sin through *adoption* into the Father's family, after the payment of a costly *ransom*: the shed blood of Jesus. Once again, it becomes clear that the means of salvation is identification with Christ. As we become united with God's only begotten Son, we share in his sonship. We too become children and heirs of the Father.

A matrix

We found, however, that sin is more than individual alienation from God and individual wrongdoing. It is a network of sick people, places and relationships—the entire, interlinked network of a disordered, Christ-rejecting culture into which we are drawn and become trapped. We are all socialized into certain sins by our culture. How does salvation undo our entrapment? It does it by helping to socialize us out of the matrix of sin, and by empowering us to bring transformation in the places where sin once held sway. The old matrix of sin is replaced with a new matrix that mediates healing and hope. Different images are used in scripture for this new matrix.

The family of God

Salvation is not simply a matter of God saving individuals, who then sit twiddling their thumbs waiting for heaven. The New Testament writers make it clear that to be a Christian is to be part of a believing community, 'members of God's household' (Ephesians 3:15). When God adopts me, I am not an only child: I become a member of a family. And it is in this new family that I learn a whole new way of living and relating.

The body of Christ

Paul compares the Church to a single body, which has many parts to it (1 Corinthians 12:12–31). Salvation draws believers into this 'body', where we learn a new pattern of collaborative living, and each contribute our gifts for the good of all. The body is a central metaphor in the letter to the Ephesians, where the sins referred to are not so much individual sins, but sins that damage the body: lying, anger, stealing, bitterness, slander, malice (Ephesians 4:25–31). The body of Christ is to be the place where people become socialized into an alternative to the matrix of sin. It is to be a place where we learn to follow Paul's exhortation to 'be kind and compassionate to one another, forgiving each other just as in Christ God forgave you' (Ephesians 4:32), to become a whole community revitalized by the power of God.

It is vital that each of us is part of a supportive Christian fellowship, where we can learn to love and be loved, share, forgive and be forgiven, and see modelled an alternative community to the matrix of sin. Without this alternative network, the journey of faith will be at best a lonely struggle. At worst, the sin matrix will simply suck us back in. As part of the body, we are stronger to resist. The most depressing scenario of all is a compromised and ineffectual church which shares the basic values of the matrix and so is unable to challenge its values head-on. The church must be a radical counter-culture, a secure base for full-scale attacks on the matrix of sin and its deceits.

The Kingdom of God

The Kingdom of God is Jesus' favourite way of speaking in the Gospels about salvation. But what is this Kingdom? Essentially, it means the rule of God, a state of affairs in which God's perfect will is done and his *shalom* reigns in all relationships. Left to our own devices, we could never be citizens of this Kingdom. Instead, due to our sin, we belong to the kingdom of the world (Revelation 11:15). But as those united with Christ, our old nature is put to death. We share in the nature of Christ, who alone can live as a true citizen of God's rule because he is God's own Son.

The Kingdom is much more than just the rule of God in my own life. It is a broad, inclusive vision of the kingship of God over the whole earth. If I am a citizen of the Kingdom, I am to pray—in the words of the Lord's Prayer—for God's Kingdom to come, and his will to be done, here, as it is in heaven. So the New Testament is filled with gritty, real-life examples of what life in the Kingdom looks like: such as Jesus' challenging Sermon on the Mount (Matthew 5—7), and his devastating parable of the sheep and goats (Matthew 25:31–46). Christians are not to be passive and resigned to the status quo, nor to wring their hands over (or even welcome) evidence of social decline. No; to experience salvation is to enlist as a member of the people of God. It is to become a person who works to see the Kingdom come, not only in individual hearts and lives, but in families, communities, companies and nations. We are not only to launch attacks on the values embodied by the matrix of sin, we are to love and bring healing to its victims, and work for its transformation.

Missing the mark

We have seen how a common biblical image for sin is missing the mark. But as we identify with the life and death of Jesus Christ, something changes here too. The word that describes this change is *justification*.

Justification

To be 'justified' means to be in a right relationship with God. The background to justification can be found in the idea of 'righteousness', although the English language obscures the connection (the Greek for 'justify' is *dikaioo*; 'righteousness' is *dikaiosune*). For somebody to be 'justified' is to be seen as righteous in God's eyes. A righteous person is not so much a person who acts in a moral way, although it can include this. It is more that he is 'right with God', in fellowship with him. Through sin, we can have no righteousness of our own before God. We are alienated from him; we miss the mark.

But Paul says that an important dimension of salvation is that God gives us the righteousness of Christ. In other words, God 'justifies' us. As we identify with Christ, we share Christ's own status before God. This is the meaning of Paul's statement that 'just as through the disobedience of the one man the many were made sinners, so also through the obedience of the one man the many will be made righteous' (Romans 5:19), and it explains his language of believers being 'justified by faith' (Galatians 3:24). This is all an extension of our being 'in Christ'. We share Jesus Christ's own standing as a righteous person, as a family member. We can finally hit that target.

Lawbreaking

The final aspect of sin we noted in Chapter 3 was the breaking of God's moral law. These are the daily sins of omission and commission we all find ourselves doing—some bigger, some smaller. How does our salvation in Christ help us handle these sins, and begin to master them? The New Testament gives us a range of clues.

Loving and imitating Christ

Jesus told his followers, 'If you love me, you will obey what I command' (John 14:15). The implications of this simple little statement are profound and far-reaching. Some people find that their main motivation for trying to live God's way and avoiding sin is duty, guilt or fear. And some Christians seem to live on a permanent guilt-trip, filled with self-loathing at their personal failures. But, as we all know from experience, actions provoked by anxiety and coercion are joyless and unsustainable. They actually end up accelerating the downward spiral. So Christ replaces the whole sorry business of legalism and fear with relationship. Love motivates where law fails. The result is that we become fired up with a *desire* to imitate the pattern of Christ's own life.

We earlier rejected the theory that following the moral example of Christ is the full meaning of salvation. As we have seen, salvation is about so identifying with Christ in his death and resurrection that we too experience a death to the old self and become a 'new creation' (2 Corinthians 5:17).

However, once we are 'in Christ', Paul makes it clear that this is not the end of the story. We are to work at becoming more like Christ in every area of our lives: such as accepting one another (Romans 15:7), forgiving (Ephesians 4:32) and loving (John 13:34). We can grow in the Christian life as we imitate the pattern of Christ's life. We are already identified with Christ, by virtue of being believers. But over time we can also be gradually more transformed into the likeness of Christ (2 Corinthians 3:18), actually becoming more like the one we love, in our thoughts and actions.

Needless to say, imitating Christ does not mean that we lose our own individual distinctives. The paradox is that as we become more like Christ, the perfect man, the more we discover our own true potential, our own distinct calling. It is sin that limits our potential, holds us back and blurs our unique distinctives. To go deeper into sin is to move deeper under the control of an alien power. But to imitate Christ is to be liberated to be who I really am.

The power of the Spirit

God does not leave us alone in our struggle with sin. He sends his Holy Spirit into our lives, to empower us to live his way. The Christian lifestyle is to be a Spirit-led lifestyle. 'Live by the Spirit,' says Paul, 'and you will not gratify the desires of the sinful nature' (Galatians 5:16).

The Spirit is our power for Christian living, helping us discern God's will, reeducating our desires (Romans 8). An important dimension to winning the inner victory over habitual sin is the resources of God's indwelling Spirit, empowering us to do what we could not do for ourselves. It is important that we pray regularly for God to pour out on us an ever greater measure of his Spirit. We desperately need to be plugged into a power greater than our own. But accessing this power must never be simply to give us a selfish spiritual high—it is to help us in the battle against sin, and in living God's way.

Self-discipline

Paul's testimony is that the Jewish Law is fulfilled in Jesus Christ, so Christians are no longer bound by the detail of the legal codes in the Old Testament. But for the believer, the external law is replaced with a new, internal obligation that calls for self-discipline. Paul compares the Christian to an athlete who has to prepare for a competition (1 Corinthians 9:27). He lists self-control among the 'fruit' of the Spirit available to us in Christ (Galatians 5:23), and tells Timothy that God gives the Christian 'a spirit of power, of love and of self-discipline' (2 Timothy 1:7).

An important part of overcoming habitual sins such as anger, greed and lust is to pray for more of this self-discipline, because for many of us it doesn't come naturally. If I could kick the backside of the person who has led me deepest into temptation and sin, I wouldn't be able to sit down for a week. In a culture fuelled by instant gratification, the biblical call to self-discipline is hard. But the rewards of persevering are worth it. The Olympic athlete trains intensively; the virtuoso musician practises daily. But these disciplines, which could be seen as irritating impositions, are essential for anybody who wants to reach the winner's podium or concert hall. Self-discipline liberates potential—not only in sport and music, but in lifestyle too.

The community of faith

We noted above, in our discussion of sin as a matrix, that God calls us not to be isolated believers, but to be members of the people of God, the body of Christ. Consequently, the New Testament assumption is that the Christian life is lived in community. We are to love each other, bear with each other's failings, and help each other along the journey of faith.

A few winters back, we had some heavy snowfalls. At the time we were living in a college house in Nottingham, which looked out over the trees in the college grounds. Some of these trees were grouped together, others standing alone. When the snow fell for days on end, it landed not just on the ground but on the trees too, the weight of the snow making them bend over further and further. Where the trees were clustered in groves, they bowed over so that the branches from one tree leaned against the trunk or branches of another tree. But where the trees were standing by themselves, one of two things happened. Either they were weighed down so far that their trunks snapped, or else they bent over so far that they couldn't be pulled upright again. Their tops had to be chopped off so that the rest of the tree could rise up again.

We're not so different from those trees. If we stand alone, we'll snap when the snows begin to fall. But if we stand together, like the trees in groves, we'll be able to lean on each other.

Become what you are

One big assumption has remained implicit in all we have said in this chapter, although we have touched on it earlier in the book. We now need to make this explicit, as it is crucial to our understanding of salvation. We have been talking about two quite different dimensions of Christ's victory over sin. But until now, we have mixed the two up together.

The first dimension has to do with our standing before God. Under this heading, we can say that in Christ we are regenerated (pp. 144–145), reconciled (p. 145), and adopted (pp. 145–146). We are liberated (pp. 146–147), ransomed and redeemed (pp. 147–148) from the power of sin. We become members of God's family (p. 149), the body of Christ (pp. 149–150) and citizens of the Kingdom (pp. 150–151). We are also justified (p. 151) as we share in the righteousness of Christ. All this happens as a birthright for the Christian who is 'in Christ'. We can't earn any of these gifts—by good behaviour, spiritual discipline or any other human work. We contribute nothing at all, beyond a simple 'yes' of faith, and by willing to be identified with the death and resurrection of Christ in baptism. It is all the sheer gift of God.

But the other dimension of salvation is quite different. It is the hard, ongoing work of discipleship, the messy work of living out our salvation in the real world, wrestling with persistent temptations, habits and compulsions. Many find it hard to reconcile the biblical language of Christ's victory over defeated sin with their own daily struggle against sins that remain all too powerful. The reason is that these are two different, but related, things. It might be helpful to distinguish them by calling them different names, such as *becoming* a Christian, and *living* the Christian life; or salvation and discipleship. The Reformers of the 16th century separated the two things out by calling them 'justification' and 'sanctification'.

All the imagery of being adopted into God's family, being liberated, justified, and so on, is to do with my becoming a Christian. As a person united with Christ, I automatically have all these benefits as a free gift from God. But at the same time, there is the other dimension of salvation: living out my faith in the world. And this is something less automatic.

I still struggle with the old human nature which keeps refusing to die, and keeps trying to reassert itself. The Christian is the battleground of the two ways to be human. I live out in myself the paradox that my sin is no longer a problem in an absolute sense, but my sins cause me difficulties on a daily basis. The good news is that these sins are already forgiven in Christ, so I needn't worry that they come between me and God. My salvation doesn't depend on my achieving a certain level of moral goodness—thank God! But believers are still called by God to lives of holiness. As somebody called to imitate Christ and live by his Spirit, I can't be content with a life where my ingrained and habitual sins are winning all the skirmishes. Victory over sin is a status that God has already given me in Christ. Now it needs to become a daily reality in my own experience, too. But how can this become more than pious optimism?

Our resources in this ongoing struggle include learning to love and imitate Christ (pp. 152–153), live by the Spirit (p. 153), acquire self-discipline (pp. 153–154), and receive the support along the journey within the Christian community (p. 154). We also have Paul's assurance that because God is faithful, he won't let us be tested beyond what we can take (1 Corinthians 10:13).

Still, the matrix of sin (p. 149) remains strong in our fallen world. And the Kingdom of God (pp. 150–151) has not yet come fully. In one sense, the reign of God begins in the life of the believer the moment they identify with Christ. The Kingdom is 'already'. But in another sense, the Kingdom is also 'not yet'. It has not yet come in its fullness, either in my own life or in society as a whole. The reign of God is something we are invited to pray and work for, as well as a wonderful birthright. It remains a struggle, as does our battle with the very real forces of evil in our world. Satan may be a defeated enemy, but he is still thrashing around causing as much havoc as he can before his final, certain demise (Revelation 12:12).

So Christian salvation has two dimensions to it. It is a present reality for every believer, but it is also a daily pilgrimage. Perhaps the best phrase to describe the ongoing journey of the Christian life is: 'Become what you are'.

What we are, objectively, is people 'in Christ', adopted, justified, liberated—the whole package. That is how Paul can claim that believers have 'died to sin' (Romans 6:2), and been set free from sin (Romans 6:18). This is quite true, in the sense that sin no longer causes the road-block between us and God. On the cross on Good Friday, sin was put to death. In the empty tomb on Easter Monday, humanity was raised to new life. And we can participate in that new life simply by saying 'Yes' to it.

Equally, anybody committed to living the Christian life knows for themselves how hard it can be. Sin may have been conquered, but we still live in a fallen world. We still struggle with doubt, alienation, bad habits, distorted relationships. The tempter is still at large. We participate in structures of injustice and oppression. The challenge for me, as a believer, is to become in daily reality what I already am in the eyes of

God. Some days I make good progress, victory seems close, and the Christian life has its moments of pure ecstasy. Other days I slip backwards, and feel an utter failure.

One thing is for sure: this struggle to uproot sin is a lifetime's job. Sometimes the struggle will seem so hard that I might feel like giving up altogether. But I am not in this alone. I have all the resources of God himself at my disposal, and there are fellow pilgrims along the way to share my burdens.

Feeding snakes

Let's be honest. To some people, all our talk of mutual support, imitating Christ, the power of the Spirit, self-discipline and so on will sound fine in theory. Many Christians will read these proposals and agree with them, but still find that the victory against sin is more theoretical than actual. The reality of countless believers' lives is that they know their sin is forgiven in Christ, but their daily life is a catalogue of moral and relational failure. In their daily skirmishes against sins of lust, greed, anger, or an addiction, the sin appears to win out every time. For all their faith in God, and belief in the power of the Spirit, they feel utterly powerless.

The reality is that people in this type of situation will never begin to see victories against sin as long as their focus is on the sin itself. They need to be gripped by a vision that is bigger and more wonderful than the temporary and limited high offered by the sin. A girl who sat at night trying to remove the darkness from her room would be doomed to failure and frustration. Darkness is only driven out when the sun rises and fills that room with light. Hope comes from opening the curtains as dawn breaks. Believers struggling with a besetting sin won't get far if they worry away at the sin itself. Hope will only come as something bigger and better floods into their soul. The heart of this 'something' lies in a real and intimate encounter with God in our daily lives. But it also needs to include a vision of ourselves as we could be in the future, a vision of the 'me' that will be the product of all the little choices I am making every day.

Most of us overvalue the instant and undervalue the gradual. This applies particularly in our spiritual and moral lives. That is why so many of us go around looking for the 'big experience' that will forever zap our doubts and wayward thoughts. We assume that if things are to be put right, it will have to be through a sudden, overwhelming experience that dramatically changes everything. This expectation is encouraged by the fact that the sudden and dramatic makes for livelier newspaper articles and Christian paperbacks. We are led to expect the 'quick fix' as the normal Christian life. Sometimes such instant solutions are forthcoming, but for most of us these are the exception. The real work of discipleship takes a lifetime.

An American family, the Romeros, bought Sally, a Burmese python, as a family pet when she was just one foot long. Each day they fed Sally and looked after her as a loved family member. Eight years later, Sally had grown to eleven-and-a-half feet, and weighed 80 pounds. On 20 July 1993, Sally turned on the Romeros' son, fifteen-year-old Derek, and suffocated him. The police who arrived at the scene reported that the snake was 'quite aggressive, hissing and reacting'.

Each time we feed a sin, we are throwing another little snack to a growing snake. And a deadly snake that is full-grown will eventually turn and destroy the one who has been feeding it. The destruction wreaked by sin includes the erosion of our zest and appetite for life, a moral paralysis in which we feel unable to choose to do right any longer, the death of relationships and trust, a growing indifference towards God, even physical death itself (through drugs, suicide, murder, and so on). When Paul warns that the wages (the just and inevitable consequences) of sin is death (Romans 6:23), he is not only giving an important spiritual truth—he is stating a simple sociological fact.

Does this mean, then, that if a Christian believer finds himself unable to stop feeding the sin snake, the snake wins in the end? That the wiles of the snake are greater than God's grace? Not a bit of it. Though we often fail, God does not easily let us go. He knows how to find lost children and bring them home, and the last word will not be the seductions of the snake, but the faithful promises of God. No snake has the power to keep God's children outside his house for ever. Look again at the Bible: God's

Kingdom is built with murderers, adulterers, swindlers, prostitutes and the weak in faith.

No, the snake will never have the last word. But a lifetime of daily feeding the sin snake will have two consequences for me. The first affects my lifestyle. I miss out on the fullness of life God intends for me. I accept second best, contenting myself with tacky substitutes for real love, joy and peace, when the real thing is on offer. And not only is sin second best, sin damages me. As we have noted, sin kills off whole areas of our lives, including our relationships, our sense of wonder and our capacity for making right judgments. Many people will finally stand before God, at the end of their lives, covered with the scars and bruises inflicted by the sin snake, its venom still in their veins. My sin cannot finally separate me from the love of God, but it can wreck my life.

The second consequence of feeding the sin snake is what it does to my love for God. The act of feeding that snake can have a profound effect on me, changing me into somebody who is no longer so interested in being a part of God's family. After a while, I stop even wanting God's love and forgiveness, especially if returning involves repenting. Here is the ultimate danger of daily feeding the sin snake: it hardens me into the sort of person who says 'No' to God. Feeding snakes is a deadly activity.

Feeding our children

But there are other individuals in our homes who can also be given food daily, such as our growing children. The day arrives when grown-up children leave home. We wonder how they changed from being that small, helpless baby to a healthy, intelligent, independent individual ready to make their own way in the world. The answer is that the change didn't happen suddenly or dramatically. It happened slowly, one day at a time, one meal at a time. The same is true of our spiritual and moral growth. It happens one decision at a time. Many times each day we choose what, or whom, we feed. Will we feed sins such as envy, greed, or lust? Or will we feed virtues such as self-sacrifice, faithfulness, and compassion? What we feed each day will either grow up and make us proud, or it will turn and suffocate us.

Our focus needs to be not so much on our sins, but on a vision of ourselves as we could be one day: a man or woman shaped by a lifetime of right or wrong choices, after a lifetime of feeding snakes or feeding our children. And, ultimately, our focus needs to be not on our sins, but on the One who has conquered sin: the passionate and compassionate Father who, in Christ, draws us into his family and sends his Spirit to be our strengthener and guide.